# PRAISE FOR FLAWE... BUT WILLING

"Khurshed is my friend and he is a true friend of the human endeavour in the workplace. And perhaps most importantly he is no friend of corporate pretence, arrogance or nonsense. It is just as well as our daily battle is to rid ourselves of it."

**CLAIRE GENKAI BREEZE**, CO-FOUNDER RELUME LTD, CO-AUTHOR, THE CHALLENGER SPIRIT

"Reading Flawed but Willing is like looking into a portal of unexpressed possibility. The stories generate powerful insights, whispering of a greater connection or a long-forgotten simplicity. The act of reading and reflecting triggered intuitive memories and ideas for alternative conversations in corporate life. It was both provocative and affirming in equal measure."

**KRIS WEBB**, SENIOR VICE PRESIDENT HR, GLAXOSMITHKLINE

"Khurshed writes fantastically provocative enquiries into corporate behaviour. Observations on our behaviour, which return the gaze of the viewer. If you have an inclination that what you are doing is not connecting in the way you want it to, or feel there is a superficiality to your corporate life, this is a great book for looking at the reflection of your leadership; a book that asks great questions of the reader, which I have found difficult to answer in a meaningful way. It also helps with the learning about what to change. The answers you need to provide for yourself, but at least you have a chance of getting closer to your own version of the truth. My recommendation is to read this book slowly, with time to ruminate. It's accessible, curious, playful, at times artistic, a great source of debate and above all helpful."

**PAUL HUNTER**, CHIEF OF STAFF TO GROUP CEO, HEWLETT PACKARD

"For me, a hugely powerful and impactful work. And at times it did feel a little hard sticking with it and not getting hooked by the very different approach to the composition and structure, but I yanked myself back into it knowing there was "gold" there for me. The power of personal experiences shared, very real, unglossy and at times disorientating in terms of where is this taking me, was immensely powerful. I loved the fact it was not simplified, boiled down to some sound-bite essence of high-level principle narrative, overall I revelled in the richness and the deliberate messiness of it, because the truth is it matches my experience of what it's like to take on myself, my team and organization in creating a new way of leading and being led, based on purposeful connectedness. It was stimulating, challenging, moving, satisfying, troubling, motivating, energising and mindset-changing all in good measure. For someone who is committed to a whole new way of purposeful and extraordinary leadership in and by business this work is a generous, but not cost-free, gift! The second half of the book , and the practice sections and questions. seem to me absolutely priceless in their value of assisting in navigating a personal and collective way through the creation of a new way. I know this book has already made a very real difference to me, and I truly sense the impact has only just begun. A heartfelt 'thank you Khurshed' for giving of yourself and providing access to others' experiences in this way!"

**STUART FLETCHER**, GROUP CEO, BUPA

**"In Flawed but Willing, Khurshed challenges me through his insights, reflections and stories to champion a new way of leading, working and being. He paints wonderfully vivid pictures of the damage we are unintentionally doing to our organizations, our teams, and ourselves by applying traditional, controlling leadership approaches in our new increasingly complex, competitive, connected world. To transition from the old to the new we have to look into ourselves, and change. We are challenged, and gently guided through the transition into the Age of Connection, where love with power, gentleness with challenge, sensitivity with strength, enable us to thrive in our new connected world."**

**CATH LYNN**, GLOBAL COMMERCIAL DIRECTOR, EASYJET

"Khurshed reminds us of the nature of discomfort required to truly lead and, I hope for many, the habit of celebrating the imperfection and messiness of such moments. Flawed but Willing - an encouragement to all who might have chosen to play safe for too long."

**GORDON BALLANTYNE**, GROUP EXECUTIVE, TELSTRA RETAIL

**"Flawed But Willing is a great sequel to The Challenger Spirit, illuminating the pathway to becoming a challenger. Khurshed's agenda is personal: an emotional rollercoaster that depresses, provokes, confuses and shocks, but ultimately uplifts the reader. The searing honesty is rare, infectious ... and potentially life-changing."**

**JONATHAN CORMACK**, GLOBAL DIRECTOR, ORGANIZATION CAPABILITY, IMPERIAL TOBACCO

"Is this a standard business / leadership book? No. Is it a useful book? I'm not sure yet, but I think it can be. Is it an interesting book? Absolutely. It could be described as an indulgence. But often when allowing another's indulgence we can take enjoyment in it ourselves: seeing the delight on your child's face when they eat the ice cream they didn't really need. In an age when you bring yourself to work and find there is no longer a 'cookie-cutter' leader or leadership style I found insightful and valuable (if they can be achieved) approaches here that I would want to see in an organization I work in; discovery through nonsense, intentionally putting ourselves at risk, having a strong back, and a soft front... With no apology for the oft lacking well-rounded conclusions you would expect to find in more typical writing, the reader is asked questions to provoke thought and to aid them in forming of their own views. The stories recounted are Dilbert-esque at times. When a particular tale resonated I found myself with a wry, knowing smile and the occasional heartfelt guffaw. The author could be critiqued for not always allowing the less cranially-capable to keep pace with the change of themes or the speed with which new ideas are introduced, although time spent on the questions posed throughout may alleviate this somewhat. I also found myself wanting to know more of the author's own thoughts and conclusions so that I might benefit from his thinking and intellect applied to these topics. I would consider this a fair exchange given my acceptance of being 'flawed but willing'. My primary fear for this text is that those who might benefit from it most are those most unwilling and unlikely to permit themselves the indulgence of reading this, or accept their own potential flaws and the changing environment around us (or perhaps even acknowledge that taking such a step should be something they should consider). I would urge them to take the risk."

**IAN DUNNETT**, CHIEF OF STAFF TO GROUP CEO, CO-OPERATIVE GROUP

**"The corporate bullshit word  is 'resonated'... but really, some of the stories in this book gave me 'that' feeling in the pit of my stomach...this is a gift that does something I've never seen in a business book...it describes not what we are thinking, but what we are feeling about corporate life."**

**SAM DUNN**, ORGANIZATION DEVELOPMENT, INVESTEC

"Flawed But Willing does not preach or promise to be a "how to" management guide. Instead, Khurshed creates a series of mental prompts for the reader to consider by sharing stories based on his extensive experience of working with senior executives. Khurshed's unique style is effective in enabling the reader to personalize the subject matter in a way that will help them better connect with others, deal with the messiness of true engagement in complex organizations and lead in a world that demands a new set of skills."

**ERICH GERTH**, PARTNER, GLOBAL HEAD OF BUSINESS DEVELOPMENT,
BLUEBAY ASSET MANAGEMENT

**"Flawed but Willing is more than a cracking read, it's an invitation to allow and seek out new ways of operating in today's dominant, but decaying system."**

**REBEKAH FLAHERTY**, GENERAL MANAGER, ORIGIN ENERGY

"The book is a generous act of challenge, attracting us to create a new, riskier but more rewarding relationship with our corporate worlds - and overcome the predictable dynamics that currently hold both us and the organization back from being our best selves."

**SAMANTHA KING**, GLOBAL LEAD EXECUTIVE DEVELOPMENT, STANDARD CHARTERED BANK

**"Organizations speak about innovation as their life blood, but seek to replicate or sustain success through analysis and processes that systematise their work, depersonalise teams and actually reduce individualism and innovation. Flawed but Willing glimpses the potential within as we grapple with lack of confidence and conflict in our unique thinking and the desire for conformation and reluctance to take risks. An introspective read whose ideas will grow over time if given the confidence and air time they deserve. The benefit of personal fulfilment and possibly even corporate success are worth the risks."**

**STUART DOLLOW**, PRESIDENT, TAKEDA DEVELOPMENT CENTRE US & MANAGING DIRECTOR TAKEDA DEVELOPMENT CENTRE EUROPE, TAKEDA PHARMACEUTICALS

"Our children will not be prepared to be managed and led in the same way that we have been. How long until the next generation creates a revolution? Khurshed eloquently describes how we need to be as leaders in this new world."

**GIFFORD TANSER**, HEAD OF CORPORATE ORGANIZATIONAL DEVELOPMENT, BOEHRINGER INGELHEIM

# Flawed but
# WILLING

# Flawed but WILLING

## LEADING LARGE ORGANIZATIONS
### IN THE AGE OF CONNECTION

**KHURSHED DEHNUGARA**

**LONDON**    **NEW YORK**    **SHANGHAI**
**MADRID**    **BARCELONA**    **BOGOTA**
**MEXICO CITY**    **MONTERREY**    **BUENOS AIRES**

**LID Publishing Ltd**

Garden Studios

71-75 Shelton Street

Covent Garden

London

WC2H 9JQ

info@lidpublishing.com

www.lidpublishing.com

A member of:

www.businesspublishersroundtable.com

Printed in Great Britain by TJ International

ISBN: 978-1-907794-77-3
Cover photography: Karen Foster
Cover design: Karin Dehnugara and Laura Hawkins
Page design:  Laura Hawkins

**FOR KARIN, ELLA AND INEZ**

# CON TENTS

A setting of expectations for intent, tone and the story-based writing style. The most challenging part may be that, although there is a point of view expressed here, there is less completion or resolution than in a standard business book.

**PART ONE**
The first part of the book uses a range of personal experiences and stories from inside organizational life to explore why this topic matters now and why it deserves attention.

Sets up the coming post-industrial age in a simple, personal way. A time when the exertion of power is shifting from the top-down hierarchy to the individual's capacity to make connections in all directions.

Tells stories about the Industrial Age logic and behaviour of today's companies/leaders and questions the relevance of the values inherent in them.

# ACKNOWLEDGEMENTS

This is a business book written as a love story. On many levels. As with all real love stories it has its beautiful, sometimes sentimental, origins, its confusions and secrets, dark parts and difficulties but I hope above all many moments of tenderness. It is an expression of my love for my wife and family, for the colleagues and clients, partners and teachers that have been kind, generous and forgiving along the way.

In particular on this book Karin Dehnugara, Brian Harrison, Karen Foster and Laura Hawkins have been the creative force behind the cover and design. Laura's editing colleagues at LID Publishing, David Woods and Martin Liu have been all that I could wish for in a publishing partner. Becky Kemp hand-made the wooden dolls we have grown to love. Karen Foster put up with countless changes of mind as she prepared the many versions of the manuscript.

The process of writing this book meant I also had company along the way from a small army of willing reviewers and critics. They were the chief encouragement officers that any venture like this requires, giving their time to read and comment as each chapter was sent in draft form to them: Anne Augustine, Gordon Ballantyne, Mandy Bennett, Sharon Brownie, Steve Chapman, Jonathan Cormack, Andrew Coull, Martin Crook, Stuart Dollow, Sam Dunn, Stuart Fletcher, Hilary Gallo, Paul Geddes, Rowan Gray, Mike Haffenden, Brian Harrison, Paul Hunter, Steve Hurst, Anne Marie McEwan, Rob Jones, Jeremy Keeley, Samantha King, Cath Lynn, Mark Martin, Nick Mabey, Stephen Fitzpatrick, Stewart Morgan, Peter O'Donnell, Rebekah O'Flaherty, Rob Poynton, Kris Webb, Kevin Page, Ann Paul, James Seed, Caroline Sharley, Craig Sked, Gifford Tanser, Russell Taylor, Perry Timms, Neil Usher, David Young, Marshall Young, Mike Young and Theodore Zeldin.

I intentionally chose an unknown and relatively junior executive to write the foreword. Matthew Tutty is an expression of the future in the present. I have great hope for the next age of our organizations when I meet people like him.

Finally, Claire Genkai Breeze is the person who had faith in me 15 years ago to do this work, she took a big gamble on someone who was full of flaws and the will to be someone different in the workplace. She is an inspiration.

**KHURSHED DEHNUGARA**
SEPTEMBER 2014

# FORE WORD

She preserves a first edition of Tolstoy's *War and Peace,* which she has read twice in the original Russian, and sleeps five hours a night to remain in constant contact with three continents.

His powerful vision has taken the company to new heights that reveal prescience for the market coursing through his veins. Ascending the mountain is treacherous, but these superhuman forces of nature are boundless. They are, after all, giants. They are leaders in the Digital Age.

It is remarkable the extent to which pulp literature on leadership ultimately gravitates towards this form of elaborate pretence. It incants the Herculean stories, catalogues the styles to model, and prescribes formulae so that you too might become a giant among the ordinary. But giants are myths. The reason for their human appearance, despite prodigious stature, is the simple fact that they are fragile, mortal and flawed. The fiction of the 'enterprise giant' creates a system of privileged knowledge and control, the limits of which are set by the endurance of those oppressed by its passive command culture. This is not the stuff of creativity and infinite possibility in an age brimming with excitement. It is the stifling, arrested development of the status quo.

Khurshed Dehnugara's Flawed but Willing wastes no time in driving to the heart of human anxiety beyond the artifice of work and business. He immediately casts away the mask of professional life, and speaks instead to the people who live, wittingly or unwittingly, beneath the costumes of leadership. More specifically, he addresses those who are driven to create change from within the establishment. A mixture of autobiography, case study and research, his tone is authentic, poetic and gripping.

In his exposition, Khurshed paints a vivid springtime that some have mistakenly reduced to "a spell called the Digital Internet wielded by wizards called the Millenials". Names like 'digital' seem, to me, redolent of a consultant's white paper or something I should buy. In seeking out the heart of this axial age – this special period between civilisations during which creativity flourishes and radical questions abound – Khurshed instead invokes the Age of Connection. Now, anyone with an aversion to fluff might immediately move away from a name that rings so touchy-feely but I think it's actually quite incisive. It isolates the primal human idea that is the substance behind many features of our times. Only in the past decade or two have trends in technology and in understanding presented an armoury sufficient to challenge the dominant solutions to life that until now could not be vetoed. Business is a pimpled, indulged and self-important teenager. The Age of Connection could prove to be the passage from the adolesence of money-making and oppressive power to the adulthood of compassion and sustainable prosperity. From the outset, it is clear the author's agenda is to help us feel deeply and strongly about the world we are creating.

But before I float away into dreaming, chapters two and three jab into my stomach with visceral stories of what it means to lead in this age when the dominant logic of our organizations is simply not in step. "Stumbling through corridors without contact", any who choose to lead in large organizations, rather than just cope, might be rewarded with the crushing sense that their lonely lot is to fill a bottomless pit. Khurshed's stories are frightening novellas that, at the same time, feel very real, and although his circumspect reflections breathe optimism into their impact, it's probably not remarkable to see themes of disillusionment, isolation, impotence, and a readiness to remain within a system long after one has lost belief. I am left to wonder whether our technological hyper-connection has overtaken our emotional readiness and set us into some kind of state of alarm.

So there it is. An emergent era of staggering possibility, and an industrial logic that asks for something fundamentally incongruent from both leaders and followers. To guide the text, Khurshed draws several circles: The first circle bounds those who represent the establishment, and the second captures those who critically reject it. But it is his third circle that is most important; overlapping the first, but independent of the second, it houses those who opt to stand with one foot inside, and one foot outside, the status quo. The circle of the 'Flawed but Willing' clings to the organizational core, and its liminal space is fraught with uncertainty and despair. Its code is purposeful disruption, but its inhabitants forego the freedom of simple rebellion in order to stay connected to others. As a result, they must stumble through, often at great personal risk to reputation and security, accepting a steady state of vulnerability and discomfort. Who on earth, then, would choose this role? Those who have hope to cause positive disintegration from the inside. Those who feel the price is a pittance compared to the promise of leading an organization somewhere beyond its own imagination.

Having established the scene and its relatable hero, three circles become the grammar for a series of very practical explorations in part two. The challenges presented by the pressures of leading in large organizations are presented as if they were carefully curated archive footage in a documentary film, and each chapter deconstructs the disciplines and practices of thriving in what might otherwise seem like the fog of war. Most notably for me, the passages brought into focus a sense that the path I imagined lonely was, in fact, well-trodden. I started to wonder how many people would identify themselves as the 'Flawed but Willing' in their world. I began to reappraise where I stood across the landscape of courage and compromise. And if valiant challengers abound, how did we end up here?

We are over-managed and under-led. We are busy, but devoid of impact. We have reached the limits of individual contribution, and exhausted material supply. Business is so highly-geared and so globally competitive that it now functions solely on discretionary effort. All that's left to eke out value is the creative strength of our relationships. There will be striving in the arena, with grit and blood, and, at times, I think this book is a catharsis for the battle-weary. But in its totality, I have found a very different message. The 'Flawed but Willing' are not afflicted nor enduring. They are not consigned to an abyss of discomfort or an eternity without resolve. They are a potent group marked by vision, drive, humility and compassion. The golden thread of the text is clearly expectant: fearless, aware and gentle, true leaders will bend the arc of history to find opportunity in this brilliant age.

Through his UK practice, research and advisory firm Relume, Khurshed has worked the world over with Global 500 CEOs and executive teams, combining a meaningful knowledge of business with a profound intuition for the people and relationships that lie beneath 21st century enterprise. He might therefore have chosen to write to the formula that ensures conventional success. He might easily have invited a recognised figure to add weight to his work by preparing this foreword. He might have provided conclusions and resolve, delivering hollow satisfaction to a broad readership. Instead, Khurshed chooses to stand at the fringes of convention and write as his creed demands. He exhibits courage, with all the risk and anxiety this entails, in order to have pathos with the 'Flawed but Willing' to whom his work is dedicated. And that might be you.

In his last work, Khurshed wrote of *The Challenger Spirit* – the will to extend beyond the comfort of the status quo in order to seed the disruption necessary for true creativity. In this work, he has lived by that spirit and been brave in content and form. I believe the result is successful in many respects: it succeeds in its relatable vignettes, it succeeds in triggering emotion, it succeeds in crystalizing the conflict between the Age of Connection and the status quo, and it begins, in earnest, a process of learning to thrive as an authentic leader against this backdrop. Behold the real giants of leadership – the 'Flawed but Willing'.

**MATTHEW TUTTY**
**JUNE 2014**

# INTRO
# DUCTION

## HOW THIS ALL BEGAN

I have woken up, a little dazed, on my sofa. Strange – I thought
I had taken myself back to my bed in time to avoid falling asleep
in front of the TV. I am disorientated and my heart is beating
quite fast. I'm anxious, it's a feeling I've been carrying for a
while, I recognize the impact on my body but, in this early hour of
the morning, it is elevated somehow. All my senses are heightened
and I can hear a scratching noise. It isn't pleasant, something is
under the floorboards. I have an extreme phobia of rats; please
don't let it be a rat.

I do what I imagine a lot of scared people do: I lie frozen – absolutely still –
hoping that when I tune in again the scratching will have gone and silence
will have returned. There it is again, from a different part of the room, I dare
not put my feet on the floor. "Wake up, get up, and stop being so pathetic!"I
tell myself. There is another scratching, it is at the windows; I never got
round to buying curtains so I can see straight out into the dark early morning
outside. No-one's there, but there it is again, not a scratching now but a
tapping. I can hear it in the bedroom too. I force myself off the sofa; it takes
an enormous effort. Now what? Can't face going into the bathroom; how do
I get away from this noise? I walk into the bedroom very slowly, like I used
to when I was scared of the dark. God it's cold. I'm shivering. The bedroom
was built as an extension onto my flat so it has never warmed up to the
same temperature as the rest of the house but it has never felt this cold. Get

under the duvet, put your hands over your ears and block it all out. I'm losing it, I can't hold it together, and everything feels like it is breaking up. I hear a child's voice asking me a question, they're not speaking loudly enough, what is it? I strain my ears to hear, I don't have the answer to the question. I know that, even before I have heard the question. For some reason, this is deeply upsetting, I start crying – no, sobbing is a better description. I can't remember crying as an adult, but something about it feels right. Not sure how long I sit there like that but, as the crying eases, the scratching and tapping voices subside. It seems to happen in proportion to the amount of daylight outside and eventually, I think, I fall asleep.

## INTENTION

At the time this happened to me, no one else would have known. On the outside, I was a high- functioning senior executive with a global pharmaceutical company. I had responsibility for a portfolio of medicines with an annual revenue of hundreds of millions of pounds. I was young and had been accelerated through the ranks – until I met my manager. She was in a period of performance difficulty and had nowhere to turn, so she did what many scared leaders do and looked for someone to blame; in this case, it was me.

Looking back, I was trying to do two things that ended up tearing me apart. Determined to get results, I was pushing for risk, creativity, participation and challenge of the status quo. Determined to be a 'good boy' I was working harder and harder at pleasing my manager the best way I knew how. I was responding to increasing persecution, constraint, rules and regulations, working harder at what had brought me success in the past…

And then I snapped.

There are many people working in organizations that are experiencing something similar to what I describe above. My work in coaching and advising senior executives across the world has brought me into contact with those at the hierarchical top of organizational life. I am privileged to have a glimpse into aspects of their world they won't share with many others. They are leading industrial organizations that are running out of growth and are stuck in a terrible contradiction. They are asked to be more creative while taking no risk.

My intention, through these stories, is to make clear that many of us are struggling; that the struggle is ok and that, with enough heart, learning, persistence and awareness, we will find our way through this particular phase.

## TONE

This poem caught my attention for style and content, the stream of consciousness providing a powerful reflection of, and insight into, the world of many senior executives in the middle of the struggle we are going on to explore.

## BAREFOOT IN THE HEART, PART 3 BY NEIL USHER [1]

buried beneath the bitter earth and the splintering boards, above barely room to breathe nailed in suffocating the resounding perpetual pounding of orders being followed pride being swallowed yesterdays being tomorrowed hope being sorrowed confounding all other thought is this what power brings? but see what they bought me on my elevation a material coronation a soundproofed billet the size of docklands arena workstation carved from a marble fillet with personal shopper chauffeur chef charwallah spoon polisher cushion fluffier spectacle buffer all more mustard to impress than words can express in thanks so initially flustered I shuffle an embarrassed deck of blanks and surreptitiously learn the royal wave goes down well with the harassed hourly paid ranks I'm now by default a millionaire debonair rarely there but my PR people really care I'm a self-fulfilling prophecy my very own currency the current rate none of mine for all of yours going to put my feet up while you're on all fours no-one going to challenge me now I'm fire retardant I've read sun tzu the executive summary but who on earth is montesqueiu doesn't seem to be in the harvard business review well sodhim got a speaking coach personal coach image coach going to be aurally and morally sculpted as befitting one catapulted into olympus cronos on one side zeus on the other no excuse for failure now no sacred cow no why or what just a greatbigblowup how now where's my speech for the investors and what are these protestors doing in the way learn from lincoln now where's a modernday pinkerton when you need one but finally cast into the sunlight at last am run aground my lungs vermiculite the eyes staring starry glistening balls of kryptonite I talk but no-one listening gulping sound wandering avenues lined with the petrified ghosts of confrontation past j'accuse! choking on thin air wondering why all around breathe softly and no-one seems to notice I am there survivor syndrome imposter syndrome stockholm syndrome and a syn drum in the seventies when life had none of the dross lost my youth at a party on mykonos took a week to find my way home then through the door never left it again buried my loss beneath the same floor I can't escape in my heart I am barefoot pierced by brittle rosethorns while all around pawns pass silent on wet grass ambivalent the path sucked into the skyline cracked lifeline in the palm of my hand understand at last that all the power I ever thought I had was secondhand

This book will not suit everyone, particularly those who have come to it following more traditional writing for business audiences. My first co-authored book, *The Challenger Spirit*, was written with the business audience in mind and I followed advice earnestly from those with more experience than me, on how to do the research, analyze and present it in a way that had the greatest chance of success. Mostly, it did and we are indebted to all those who told us how much they enjoyed the writing and how much difference it made to their lives.

But, of course, the one slightly critical review we received shouted loud in my ear. This would usually have been because of my determination to drive for perfection but, this time, it was something more. It was because it was true and, in some ways in our last piece of writing, I hadn't been completely true to myself or the voice I wanted to represent. This review said (among nice things) that the writing had been over-edited, it wasn't a gripping read and that the poetry was lost as a consequence. All true.

This time around, I have approached writing in a different way. Rather than worrying about structure and form, I have simply written what comes to mind each day, following my interest and energy. Rather than conducting interviews and analyzing them, I have relied on the database that is my memory. Rather than quoting eminent business people who generously offered their insights, almost everything here is unattributed. Rather than turning stories into insights, I have left them as stories. Rather than taking myself out of the work and making it as objective as possible, I have thrown myself into the work and made it as subjective as possible.

The resulting writing is a mixture of autobiography, fiction, case study and research. It is a reflection of my life and that of my colleagues in this field. It has been written with others, not apart from them. All of it is true and all of it is untrue; all of it happened, but not exactly in the way described. In order to protect individuals, organizations and experiences I have mixed up the stories, hopefully without losing their essence.

If you read anything here and think 'he is writing about me and us' that is good enough (although I won't have been).

Given the difficult ground from which this writing originates, at times, the tone has a dark texture. At the same time, I don't believe everything that is important has to be discussed intensely or seriously. I hope very much that moments of lightness, playfulness and humour also play their part; they certainly have done in the real life experience of these stories!

Tim Smit KBE was kind enough to write the preface for our first book and called it "a bible for the Flawed but Willing". That phrase has always stayed with me and has inspired a new book title that fits the context I want to write about.

In the spirit of the Age of Connection I wrote the book as a social and transparent act, sharing the chapters publically, and early, with a group of friends, colleagues and interested strangers. The experience reinforced my own 'Flawed but Willing' state! Opinion from the reviewers was almost always split down the middle, and a flavour of this has been included at the start of each chapter as a source of stimulation and engagement with what is to come.

## LACK OF RESOLUTION [2]

Wolfgang Amadeus Mozart had an elder sister named Nannerl. She was an excellent harpsichordist and a composer. Her little brother idolised her and followed her into music. They invented a secret language that only they shared and were as thick as thieves. One little myth depicts this relationship and their characters charmingly: at the moment Nannerl appeared for dinner each evening, Wolfgang would covetously, and precociously, sit in her chair. They would argue and she would eventually prevail. One night, she arrived and, again, he sat in her chair. She walked straight past him to the fortepiano. She played a scale... every note but the last, then walked back to her chair and stood beside it patiently. Wolfgang, unable to endure the seventh of the scale hanging in the air, hurriedly vacated Nannerl's chair and ran to play the final note of the scale.

Most of us have a proclivity for story resolution, particularly from a 'business' book! And yet there is something about leaving the scale hanging that is inherent in this approach to writing. Ultimately, as a result of reading this work, I hope you feel deeply and strongly about the world we are creating, engage with your own stories, both those completed and ongoing, and rise from your chair to complete the scale with your own final note.

**KHURSHED DEHNUGARA**
SEPTEMBER 2014

# ONE

## On the cusp of a new age

---

I always want to understand the nature of the argument and ideally the answer up-front, as without it I won't want to invest my time and money in buying and reading a book which may not go anywhere or whose conclusion I instinctively disagree with. Having read the introduction and first chapter, it is clearly well written, but I only just understand the question you're trying to answer, and have no clue as to the answer.

I like it because it eschews the pretence of knowing and having an answer, which is, of course, a large part of the problem (or predicament, since the whole problem - solution language isn't helpful). I am bored with people saying "there are no magic bullets" before then presenting a bullet (framework, theory, concept, language, grid, tool etc.) which if not magic, is doing a passing imitation or can easily be understood as proto-magical by those looking to evade the uncertainty of not knowing. So I appreciate the inclusion of the mess, the uncertainty, and the non-linear poetry of it, though poetry is perhaps too polished a term, it is spiky, heartfelt, raw, jagged, awkward. Like life.

---

## THINKING ABOUT OUR ANCESTORS

Having been born in Bombay, I am grateful for the opportunity to fly back and forth to India for work; a strange mixture of emotions always hits me when the plane doors open and I submerge myself in the noise, heat, inconvenience and smell that is Delhi or Bombay. I am torn – part alien that doesn't belong, part native, coming home.

This trip has me reflecting on the way the forces governing the industrial society have been in my family for at least three generations. My grandfathers were part of the British Empire in India and Kenya; they would have experienced the creation and development of our Industrial Age first-hand. My paternal grandfather spent most of his time away from home helping to construct and maintain the railways that still crisscross the land, underpinning the personal and industrial connections of this enormous sub -continent. My maternal grandfather worked as an administrative clerk on the docks in Mombasa, Kenya, managing the passage of freight from India to Africa to Europe and back again. I imagine them, in their working lives, as cogs in the machines that, in many ways, began with the East India Company; maybe the world's first iteration of an Industrial Age organization. I'm sure hierarchy, management, structure, process, efficiency focus, avoidance of error and punishment were all part of their cultural norms.

My maternal grandfather used to drink a whisky with soda, play whist and name Saturday nights 'Golden Night'. It was the beginning of the one-day weekend for which the rest of the week was penance. I have a fantasy that, were I able to talk to them about their working life, it would not have sounded very different from the cultural conditions within which our organizations operate today.

My mother benefited from her parents' hard work and the generosity of family already living in England. She was able to emigrate to the UK, train as a nurse and provide some of the human capital the country desperately needed at the time. My father did the same, qualifying as a pharmacist and working in a range of roles in the pharmaceutical industry. Fast-forward a generation and we see the same cultural conditions in place in large hospital and pharmaceutical company institutions. I remember hearing my father complain, on many evenings, as he took off his suit and tie and changed into his pyjamas, about the unnecessary bureaucracy, complexity, hierarchy and prejudice against difference – whether relating to skin colour or the diversity of ideas.

In the next generation, my brother and I followed our father into the pharmaceutical world, starting as sales representatives. The high numbers of people visiting GPs and hospital doctors in those days was often referred to as the "sales and marketing machine" and, yes, you guessed it; the same cultural conditions were in place.

In my grandparents' era, workers were expected to be docile and subservient to authority, earning their place by doing what their managers told them to do, efficiently and to a high standard. There was little room in the system for their own imagination, feelings, needs or wants. Any resistance against their bosses' wishes was conducted quietly and passively, for fear of punishment. The atmosphere was one of fear, insecurity and helplessness all reducing the cultural health of the organization.

While conditions have changed over these three generations, perhaps they haven't changed all that much. Maybe we are just better, nowadays, at ignoring some of the difficulties and pretending they don't happen.

Will it be that way for my children, nieces and nephews? I doubt it. While a 'new age' is impacting on them mostly through the digital entertainment offered, I cannot imagine them working in the same organizational environments as currently exist. They won't tolerate it and will expect more from their parents, so now is the time of transition. For those of us 20 years in with 20 years to go before we retire - how do we need to change?

## THE AGE OF CONNECTION

I read a lot about the death of hierarchy, centralized control and managers as leaders. There are a number of very sophisticated commentators who suggest that the world of the industrial organization is over and that a new organizational structure, based on some kind of combination of Wikis, internet retailing, 3D printers and crowd funding, is the way forward. This feels a little overwhelming and unreal to me and I'm not sure the social and organizational challenges we face will all be wished away with some kind of magic spell called the Digital Internet wielded by wizards called the Millennials.

The forecasters may yet be proved right but my day-to-day experience in large industrial organizations doesn't suggest so. I suggest the more likely scenario is that we will increasingly overlay a more connected age on top of the structures currently in place. Another way of thinking about it may be that this connected paradigm has always been in place, it is just that we imposed an artificial industrial structure on top of it. Whichever you prefer, we are talking about a gradual disintegration of the old Industrial Age through integration of the new Connected Age rather than a destruction of the old and a replacement by the new.

The distinction is important.

There are many possible futures that will continue to need hierarchical and centralized approaches. My position is simply that an over-emphasis on them in the past has led to difficulties and decay, particularly in the creative and adaptive leadership that is needed for them to thrive.

Frankly, I have no idea what is coming next, I just know that there are signs of deterioration in the current paradigm and that something new is about to emerge.

If we accept we don't know what the future holds, then the 'Flawed but Willing' have to be concerned with helping the new emerge. That is the focus here. How will you unlock the door in your organization to allow these promised 'breakthroughs' to actually break through?

Our objectives in this book are to help you wake up to what is going on. We want to help you develop resilience to face the ongoing change and constant restructuring you're probably facing and learn how to thrive in this 'new age'. This is your responsibility to future generations.

Others have used the terms the 'Third Industrial Age', 'Digital Age' or 'Information Age' to describe what we are beginning. Those titles just about work, but leave me feeling a little cold.

I prefer a different title – how about the 'Age of Connection'? It tells you about the main benefit and threat of this new age and distinguishes it from what came before, which in my mind has been the age of efficient machines (and separateness).

Here is a simple table of the way organizations are integrating a new age into the old one. I am sure it is incomplete but in the spirit of the new Age of Connection it makes the point well enough.

| INDUSTRIAL AGE | Age of Connection |
|---|---|
| Machine metaphor | Environment metaphor |
| Inherently stable | Inherently unstable |
| Efficiency dominant | Adaptability dominant |
| Leader as controller | Leader as wizard |
| Control through sign-off | Control through self-policing |
| Teacher as expert | Community as expert |
| Architects | Artists |
| Perfectionism | Fast failure |
| Hierarchy | Network |
| Fleas live off elephants | Fleas can kill elephants |
| High growth, minimal fluctuation | Low growth, maximum fluctuation |
| Relatively closed-off, defended from the outside world | Highly permeable to the outside world |
| Rigid but mostly secure employment | Voluntary, flexible, insecure employment |
| Leader as jerk. Can survive and thrive across a whole career | Leader as jerk. Gets exposed and rejected quickly |
| Self-interest | Collective interest |

Since I started writing about this phenomenon, we have encountered a number of self-organizing groups which are interested in the same field. If you look to the edges of our organizational lives you can see the beginnings of a movement that we hope this book will amplify and accelerate. Here are some principles from a self-organizing movement called The Corporate Rebels United. [3]

## WHAT IS THE PROBLEM?

Our organizations no longer serve our needs. They cannot keep pace with a high-velocity, hyper-connected world. They can no longer do what we need them to do. Change is required.

## WHAT IS THE VISION?

We love our organizations and want them to succeed. We want to reboot our corporate and organizational culture to install a 21st century, digitally-native version, to accelerate positive viral change from deep within the fabric of our organizations, and to reclaim our passion for work.

- We want to build an action-driven community.
- We want to create an incredible energy bomb of corporate change.
- We aim for a very high level of integrity and authenticity. We want this to be morally, intellectually, and artistically right.
- We want to re-enforce the energy of known rebels in a non-zero sum community.
- We want to identify and unleash the energy from the hidden rebels and the hidden pearls in our organizations and give them a voice.
- We want to create exchange programmes between our corporations.
- We want to have deep, positive business impact on the corporations and organizations that host and pay our salaries.
- We want to create a culture in our corporations where change is the norm.

- We want to measure the progress and propulsion we make/create: in ourselves and the folks we influence.
- We want to evolve our corporations into places of constant change, resilience, responsiveness, reflection and vibrant energy.
- We want to create a place for play, fun, rock, and rich personal expression.

I know, I know, I read that from the part of me that is leading a machine and think "what a load of old guff". Meaningless words and hot air; written by people who will never achieve anything and don't have the first idea about how to run an organization. Then I look at the right-hand column above titled Age of Connection and read the principles again. They make much more sense now. What an exciting time to be alive.

# TWO

## Corridors without contact

- — _ - - - — - — - - — - — - — -

As for the Dominant Logic, I do not
recognize all of these in the Leaders nor
the Followers, so although a few do ring
true this seems a bit stereotypical
and as such this chapter does not really
speak to me I am afraid.

My reaction to the dominant logic almost
without exception has been, "I can believe that,
it rings wholly true, I've been there."

- — _ - - - — - — - - — - — - — -

## CORRIDORS WITHOUT CONTACT

He talks quickly and walks as fast as he talks, I have a long stride but I am half running to keep up with him. I seem to do a lot of this nowadays. He has done well in life, is inherently self-reliant and very suspicious of the value coaching may provide. As we walk through the office, he changes path every few steps to say something to one of his team in the open-plan office. A direction here, a question there and a critique of an unfortunate couple of slackers.

I wait while he delivers his piece to his team and he picks up the strand of our conversation with ease. We are only talking because his manager suggested he might wish to consider the value of doing some work with me, focusing on his superiority and extreme performance focus. "It may help your relationships and future success," his manager said. "No harm in a quick conversation."

I am torn about these types of interaction, half of me enjoys the challenge, the other half is resentful of the dance that is necessary before we can talk about anything meaningful. But I am still in the room after 40 minutes so something must be working for this time-poor senior executive to still be engaged in the conversation.

"What is it you want out of this work?" I ask. He is stumped, not sure how to answer. We sit in a comfortable silence while his brain whirrs and his eyes dart around the room; I make meaningful notes in my small new moleskin book with which I am very pleased. I thought we were at a stage of the conversation where we would get a little deeper, maybe a recent difficult experience or some pointed feedback he had received would be the beginning of our contract. We don't start there but that isn't unusual, we start somewhere a little more transactional. He wants some help preparing for the next promotion or next role elsewhere. Again, quite a common starting point, maybe not as juicy as I imagined but from these humble beginnings we often end up in memorable relationships and conversations. And then my blood runs a little colder.

"I have done well and I have a lot of the things I wanted in terms of what money can buy but the next job has to be the big one."
"What do you mean by 'big one'?"
"Well, it has to be the 'f**k-off job'."
"I'm not familiar with that expression..."
"A 'f**k-off job' is the job you have which, when they tell you to f**k off, you don't have to worry about working again."

## GETTING GOING IN THE MORNING

I am taking a regular coaching session with a senior executive who has been with his multinational organization for 15 years. He was promoted quickly through the ranks and, until recently, highly-valued for his contribution. Today, his eyes are a little deadened, there isn't the spark I have come to associate with him. He does his best with the small-talk that usually accompanies the walk from reception, past security. We pick up cups of tea from the cafe and try not to spill them as we walk up the stairs and across the bridge. I find a way of wedging the door open with my foot as my bag is in one hand and the cup of tea is burning the other. Why do I never add one of those cardboard sleeve things when offered?

Listening to what he is saying to me, it is an all-too-common conversation. He describes a particular slump that has been some time in coming but from which he doesn't feel he can extricate himself. As I sit with him, I am reminded of my work as a therapist with patients who are clinically depressed. He hasn't filled in a symptom survey but I am fairly confident what the scores would indicate if he did.

"I find no joy in this role, I don't want to get up in the morning and it has been that way for a long time. When I do drag myself up, I have to face a long commute to work and the dead time in the car just seems to amplify the low energy. When I get to work it feels like I have done a day's work before I get through the office door."

I ask him about the work environment and his relationships.

"You know I thrive on innovation and intellectual stimulus, there just isn't any of that here. There could be, but I haven't been involved in the creation of a case for this project, I feel little ownership; in fact, I just don't believe in the work. When I try and voice my opinions I face hostility but it is of the passive-aggressive kind, nothing obvious that I can face up to. I don't get to complete anything to my own high standards so the job satisfaction dips further. I feel as if there is a big hole here that I have been working harder and harder to fill but it is a bottomless pit."

## SPREADSHEETS AND SNACK MACHINES

We are sitting in front of a spreadsheet that has grown in complexity many times since we first started working on it. The man next to me is a finance analyst adept at manipulating these documents; I am a commercial director trying desperately to forecast accurately a figure for our next year of sales across our portfolio of brands.

We have variables for market segmentation, penetration, competitor trends, environmental changes of which we are aware and much more. The analyst is frowning and squinting, the screen in front of us contains minute font sizes representing big numbers in terms of sales and profit.

I am so bored of this work, it takes a long round of meetings where various stakeholders have to be consulted, each of them with an expert view on what the future will look like, all fearful of predicting too low or too high. This prepares for the final show-down with the regional director for Europe who will most likely sweep in, debate the numbers for a while and then proclaim the need for 10% more of something from somewhere. We check and re-check hoping that an unseen number or equation somewhere won't make us look ridiculous at some future meeting.

The year ahead, of course, turns out to be nothing like our forecast. We take one of our regular walks to the machine which, when fed with cash, thankfully churns out a packet of crisps or a chocolate bar or a fizzy drink that will keep us going for a little longer.

Even my friendly analyst has had enough of this. "You know," he says thoughtfully, chomping through a particularly chewy bar of some kind, "a lot of this is bullshit."

## PROXIES FOR POWER

We are sitting in a large U-shaped configuration around a table, everyone has their laptop in front of them, and the cjhief executive officer (CEO) sits, intentionally, at the head of the table. There are a number of consultants in the room from one of those big consulting houses that specialize in this kind of work; each one a different grade of seniority with a different job to do.

The senior partner sits to the side of the CEO, the most junior seems to spend all day handing out documents and collecting them in again. There is a £50 million saving to be found and the day will be a long one. There are thick folders of paper next to the laptops to which we refer occasionally: *"You'll see in the table on page..."*

The consultants have been brought in because the executive team cannot identify the savings to be made and balance the resource allocation across the business strategically for its changing context. Each team member is asked, in turn, to present their proposals for examination by their colleagues.

The big, growly chief operating officer (COO), who holds a big proportion of the spend, is in full flow. It is hard to stop him speaking, never mind challenge what is being presented.

He treats resource allocation as if it is a proxy for power: if you have the most people, the biggest spend, you must be higher in status than everyone else. Don't dare imagine that your part of the business may be starting to fade, keep hold of the resources for as long as you can; find more time for your team to prove that the work is valuable; and point anywhere, everywhere else in order to fund new, uncertain projects that may define the future.

What are the values inherent in the stories? What do they mean? Are they still useful for the challenges we now face?

At one level, there is nothing wrong with the stories outlined above, they are an expression of the average day in many large corporations; well-intentioned, talented people going about their work doing the best they can, with what they have. I don't feel anything but empathy for the struggles these people are facing. I applaud the autonomy, power, right and ability to shape our own destinies that some of the stories suggest.

I think they serve to demonstrate the root cause of the crisis we are facing – but maybe it is more helpful to think of it in terms of a phase shift rather than a crisis. The stories speak to me of a loss of connection, limited empathic contact with our self, the people we work with, those that follow us and the needs of a wider society as a whole.

There is no doubt that, over the past 100 years, we have been widening our capacity for contact, empathy and equality in the workplace, incrementally. At the same time, it feels to me as though the progress in corporate life is stalling, if not going backwards. Under the extreme pressure of the past few years, our anxiety leads those of us working together to revert to separateness and more 'aggressive' communication with one another.

If we stall, we have little hope of bringing about the shift that we are due. We will not be able to force the next phase into fruition as we did the last one. The Industrial Age came about through superior scientific knowledge, administration and machinery. The next age is a more subtle endeavour, brought about by a self-aware, socially-embedded model that coaxes, persuades, invites, nudges, and feels its way forward. Our successful corporations, in the medium term, will be those that see themselves connected integrally to the social and natural world, rather than disconnected from it, operating as separate, wholly-autonomous entities.

It is not only about our leaders, we all have a part to play in the status quo and in changing it. The dominant logic carried around in the heads of our leaders is reinforced and kept in place by the dominant logic of those following them.

## DOMINANT LOGIC FOR LEADERS
## IN THE INDUSTRIAL AGE

- The people before us didn't know what they were doing; we will sort all that out now and diminish their reputation along the way.

- We have supreme confidence in our ability to plan for outcomes and deliver them. (Despite knowing that at least half of the outcome is dependent on forces for which we cannot account).

- If any doubt surfaces, question the quality of strategic thinking before our time. We need slicker strategic thinking. Call McKinsey or BCG.

- Don't worry about conflicting internal interests. Just champion your own and make sure you win. Above all, don't bring any lack of alignment into the open. Handle it through private, closed-door conversations.

- Activity, efficiency and output have organizational currency beyond the real value of what is produced.

- Evaluate new ideas based on the perception of the person expressing them and their skill in stakeholder management.

- Look for evidence that what we are doing is working and minimize evidence that what we are doing is not working.

- If we have invested personally in something in our past it must work, or at least we must pretend that it worked.

- Never admit to failing – especially when we've under performed, failed at innovation or failed at serving the customer.

- When we can't grow we shave another 10% from the workforce numbers. And claim success.

- If we can no longer hide the fact that we are failing then replace the CEO and remember to claim you disagreed with their leadership all the way along.

## DOMINANT LOGIC FOR FOLLOWERS IN THE INDUSTRIAL AGE

- People who are in charge and in control lead me. They have more intelligence than me. I must do as they say; they know what they are doing. I idealize them and their capabilities beyond what is realistic.
- They don't mean what they say when they ask for my input and creativity.
- I would do more, if only they would let me.
- I must identify the prevailing view and then manage myself within it.
- Being clear is a pre-requisite. I can't say I don't know what I am doing.
- If I speak up about the failings around here, I will lose my job.
- Loss of share, sales, profits and projects must be avoided at all costs, even if a little sacrifice could lead to a lot of gain.
- It is better to stay than to leave and not know what to do or how to cope. I have many reasonable reasons for holding onto my job here.

So we are left wondering which is a more appropriate dominant logic, common philosophy or set of principles for the way we could go about leading our organizations in the Age of Connection?

# THREE

## Stumbling through the transition

With respect to the liminal space concept, I understood it from your therapy descriptions but struggled with it in the organizational context. I think I understood that the place for it was in the overlap between the status quo and the challenger but didn't understand how it would be constructed, unless you were saying that for the challenger individual they would build some sort of way through here; a bit lost here I'm afraid.

I have had a read of the next chapters and I really like them. I like the personal stories in particular and I think you are being very courageous in being so open about how you experience interactions. I think this will be really useful for readers and certainly not something I have seen before.

## STUMBLING THROUGH THE TRANSITION

I am driving up the motorway again for my weekly visit to see the psychoanalyst who has been helping me to recover from my recent breakdown. It was a bit of a storm back then and I am still trying to make sense of my mother dying from cancer, my marriage breaking down and my performance at work – struggling to keep up with the demands of the corporate bully that was my boss at the time. Back then, I had no idea this kind of psychological help was available so I jumped to work with the first psychoanalyst I discovered, not thinking it would result in a two-hour round-trip every week for 10 years.

I reach for the radio and turn off the sports reporting that accompanies many of my drives. My Brentford Football Club are playing away at Colchester United this evening and I was hoping for some team news but I know that now is a time to be without distractions. Over the years, this long drive has become a way of preparing for the session on the way there and reflecting on the session on the way back. So, somehow, it becomes a three-hour session of therapy rather than one. The motorway is moderately busy, the daylight is disappearing slowly behind the Chiltern Hills and my thoughts turn to a concept introduced to me at the last session. It was the first time my therapist Jean talked about the concept of liminal space as a channel between one place and another in our psychological development.

I had been struggling for a while with how little progress we were making, my world then was one in which there was a straight and direct line between where you were and where you wanted to get to. I felt I was going round in circles during the therapy conversations: there were stories, experiences, insights, complaints, overwhelming emotions, difficult relationships but nothing was happening and I was going nowhere! I felt better, I was sure, but had no idea why or how yet.

"Explain what is going on please?" I said to her in that way where asking a question implies a statement of complaint. Subtext: "You don't know what you are doing and I am damned if I am going to keep driving up and down the motorway for someone who doesn't know what they are doing!"

The concept of the liminal space was first developed by the anthropologist Arnold van Gennep[4] and came from his examination of the ancient rituals that helped individuals and tribes move through different ages of life. He found that ancient societies had ways of being with each other and ways of working on themselves that held them together while they passed through significant periods of transition from one stage to the next.

In my personal experience, as I stood on the threshold of change, looking back at my historical way of structuring my identity, the next step was characterized by ambiguity, confusion, disorientation and iteration as I stumbled my way through.

In our work watching those in corporations leading this phase shift, as we stand at the threshold of what has been our historical way of structuring our identity, time and community, this adjacent space is also characterized by a state of ambiguity and disorientation (See Figure 1).

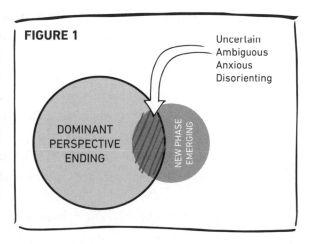

**FIGURE 1**

Uncertain
Ambiguous
Anxious
Disorienting

DOMINANT PERSPECTIVE ENDING

NEW PHASE EMERGING

I have seen, many times over the years in organizational life, that this stage of a phase shift causes people to revert even more strongly to methods that have served them well in the past. Ways of acting, habitual mindsets they hold, forms of organising the environment around them. This provides a much-needed source of security, which we hope will help us rush past the disorientating stage and into a new period of success. At the precise moment we most need the dominant perspective to loosen its grip, we allow it to exert itself more strongly.

I can't find a better way of describing what we have to do than to say it is a 'stumbling through' this part of the change that is required. That's not very corporate, I know, and not the kind of story we hear about our heroic CEOs, but it is at the heart of the work. One of my coaching clients described it as follows:

## SINKING AND SWIMMING

It is as if I sink into something, a space in which I know I can't stay forever, but that is very attractive while I am there. It doesn't sound attractive as I describe it – dark, hollow, tunnel-like with an echo.

Another way to describe it would be that I let myself sink into something that yields, but doesn't disintegrate. It was difficult to enter this mode initially as it felt too uncertain and I wasn't sure what you would make of me talking in this way but as I learned it was ok it has been responsible for some of the most helpful insights and changes in our time together.

When something shifts in this time, it doesn't shift because I force it or set myself an objective of some kind or do my homework. It is less tangible than that but still very powerful; it just happens, I can't explain it any better than that. The most significant part of the coaching, which has been a big learning process in itself, has been to give up control and defence.

When I am able to do that, I can collapse into the nothingness, the emptiness, and something new comes out of that. It sounds depressing but it isn't, it is actually quite uplifting eventually but you can't get to the very energetic part without passing through the difficult stage.

At the moment, I can't allow this anywhere else other than during our coaching sessions, so this time is precious to me. Nowadays, I become impatient when we don't access it quickly enough. Sometimes, it is as if I am floating above our conversation looking down on myself in this room, wondering what is going on. It is disorientating; at the most meaningful moments, it has felt like something is breaking down into pieces but I don't lose them. The same broken pieces reform in a new order. When I stand there, it feels very subjective, I'm frequently changing direction, having to connect unexpected ideas. I bounce around between the tangible and the abstract. I am left with questions and some patterns rather than answers. I keep aspiring and find myself, periodically, rather weary and lonely.

## THE CHANNEL

If we are to lead our organizations into the next age, we will be doing so as challengers to the status quo; connecting, sensing, experimenting, provoking and disturbing them from the edges of what is the dominant perspective. And if we are to do so, we will need to build a channel that is strong enough to hold all the anxiety we will feel and all the anxiety we will provoke in others.

In this phase, there is an overlap between the established way of doing things and the new way that is emerging. What if we thought of the overlap as a channel inside which change can be catalyzed? Change for the individual, change for the business and change for wider society. How do we build something that is strong enough to hold the powerful emotional forces that will be present; strong enough to contain without being so strong that it becomes oppressive? How do we build something that is flexible enough to bend to the unknown responses that are generated; flexible enough to allow new levels of creativity without becoming so soft that it feels unsafe?

Do give some attention to how you build your own channel. What do you have inside you and around you that will help as you stumble through from one phase to the next? (See Figure 2).

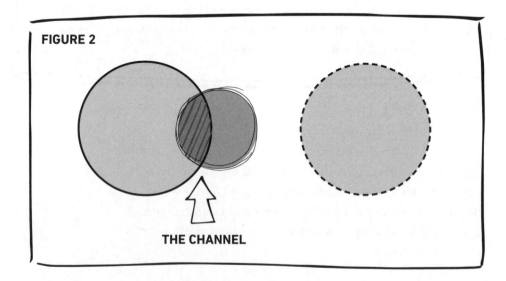

**FIGURE 2**

**THE CHANNEL**

## CALM IN THE CRUCIBLE

I am facilitating a group of leaders on a development course; the group process sessions are a crucible inside which much personal learning takes place. They are usually testing environments in which individuals learn through feedback about their part in the group dynamic. They experience, in real time, their own and others' projections, seeing, in other people, what they least wish to identify in themselves.

Today, one female participant is on the receiving end of a lot of heat. She tries, repeatedly, to draw attention to the aspect of the group dynamic that is not 'allowed in the room', something that is there but is not given space for reflection or discussion. The remaining group members turn on her, some actively, others passively. She holds her ground, calmly, reflectively, enquiring into what she feels and experiences without taking all the blame for it or depositing all the blame on others.

There are many attempts by the group to move on to another topic, shut her up and avoid the questions being posed. Usually, I would intervene or there would be some kind of drama that manifests the anxiety: tears; someone leaving the room; a challenge to the process; a group member turning on the facilitator; a complaint about the course; or all the above. Not this time. The conversation continues through its twists and turns, needing no intervention from me and concludes with learning and insight for all involved.

I asked the protagonist afterwards what enabled this way of being. "I think putting myself in therapy for a while.... I learned to experience the extreme anxiety I had been avoiding for most of my life and how to work with it rather than suppress it."

# FOUR

## Flawed but willing

Well that was a rich read this morning. Those vignettes are like the cuts of a film you know. They each have drama, a twist and a lot of characterization. They are also slightly dream-like. I think there is a bit of a jar between these stories and the propositional text. It is not a big thing but it left me wondering if there was a way to make a bridge between the two states for the reader. A sort of momentary pause to connect with my own memories of similar experiences. Resonating or disagreeing from my experience before moving into your insights?

Coming to the boil beautifully now. Your anecdotes, reminiscences, etc are remarkably effective at rapidly moving on the line of argument (telegraphing what in standard biz books would take multiple pages of blurb). Very well chosen .

## CONSTRAINTS AND OVERLAPPING CIRCLES

I am wondering if I have finally hit the big time. My fees for speaking to conferences aren't significant but this organizer has told me that there is some good news and bad news. The good news is that I am still speaking; the bad news comes in stages, as I peer into the gloom behind the production desk that is scrambling desperately to get this conference on the road.

The ash cloud (caused by the Icelandic volcano eruption which disrupted flights across Europe) has meant we have lost a substantial part of the 300-strong audience (not literally they just haven't arrived) and much of the production equipment.

"I can get you a microphone but nothing else, so no slides no background support of any kind".
"Ok," I say gamely, thinking how to shift things around.
"Oh, and by the way we can only give you 20 minutes".
"Ah," I say, slightly less enthusiastically,having prepared a two-hour session.

It was another part of my brain that was calculating my fee divided by 20 minutes to see if I was now in the region of the supermodels who claimed they wouldn't get out of bed for less than an exorbitant amount per day.

"Did we get the paper tablecloths?" I enquire.
"Yes," he says, rather gruffly.

I imagine he wished some of his kit had made it there at the expense of our tablecloths. But, fortunately, they gave us the option of allowing our audience to draw on the cloths and capture their insights. It was this constraint that generated the three circles we will be using through the rest of the book.

As constraints often do, they generated, in this case, a creative output and one that yielded plenty of interaction and insight. We talked at length about how to lead this phase shift in our organizational lives:

- If we weren't to fall victim to the changes but lead them.
- What if we were able to pick up the signals of the future when they were small enough to do work with creatively?
- What it means to represent a challenge - standing with one foot inside and one foot outside the status quo. (See Figure 3)

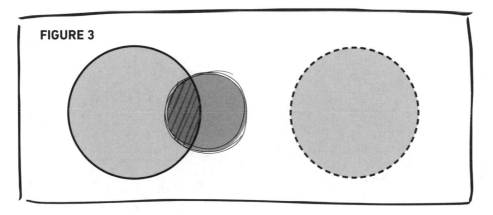

**FIGURE 3**

How this position was a constantly dynamic one, working out how you ever know whether you are too far in or too far out.

What distinguished being a Challenger from being a Rebel and how easy it was to end up being tipped from one position to another.

Not bad for 20 minutes,
Thank you ash cloud.

## THE ESTABLISHMENT, CURRENT REALITY, STATUS QUO, DOMINANT LOGIC

In this place (see figure 4) we have the majority of those that occupy leadership roles in our largest industrial organizations. They are mostly well-intentioned and committed to ensuring the success of their businesses and the security of the people who follow them. At their best, they also turn their minds to how their business can benefit society more widely.

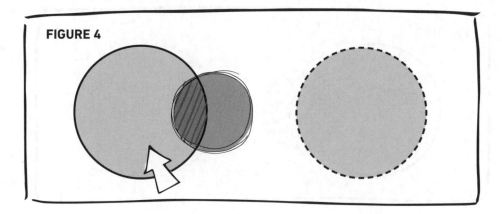

**FIGURE 4**

The organizations for which they are responsible value quarterly profit numbers, growth and share price, they have immense individual and collective power and yet, in their quieter moments, they would admit to various degrees of insecurity. Are they good enough? Will they survive? Do others in positions of power regard them positively? When will they earn enough money to earn the right to relax from the pressure they put on themselves?

In this population, there is also an increasing sense of meaninglessness that arises from the short-lived delights of material wealth. They are often lonely, dissatisfied and questioning the purpose of their lives. They have mostly achieved the definition of what a successful life looks like. It is one that has been drilled into them through their family, school, social and professional relationships.

## THE REBEL, ANARCHIST, DROP-OUT, PROTESTOR

At the other end is a population that may still be in the organization or may have left for another life. (See figure 5) If they can't possess the success of those in the Establishment or abhor the values in use over there they leave themselves with only one choice - to exit. This might be an emotional exit, a physical one or both.

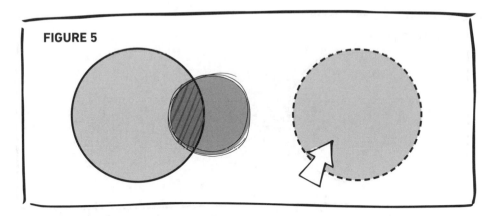

**FIGURE 5**

From wherever they are they can project onto their (sometimes former) organizations and those working in them a sense that they are wrong and the world can only benefit by the destruction or removal or diminishment of corporations as they currently exist.

## THE FLAWED BUT WILLING

In the middle smallest circle are our Flawed but Willing. (See Figure 6) They recognize the flaws in the system and in themselves, they have some hope of shifting the businesses and people they love to a place where they may be able make the transition to a new Age of Connection.

Rather than accepting the status quo or trying to destroy it they are looking to work compassionately inside it, causing a positive disintegration from the inside; often doing so despite the risk of damage to their reputation and security.

They are described in a range of ways: the challenger, facilitator, emergent leader, intrapreneur, whistleblower, channel opener and sometimes all of the above!

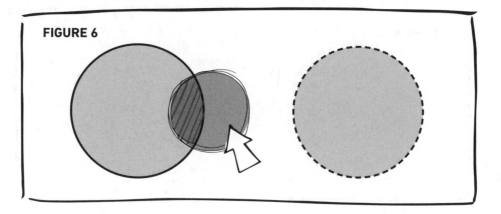

**FIGURE 6**

They develop a new relationship between themselves and their work as we will see in the rest of this writing; touching feelings of inadequacy, longings of the heart, despair, sweet ,short-lived moments of breakthrough, hopelessness, delight and dissatisfaction.

Through their work they come to acknowledge their deep fear of change, especially if that change has a potential impact on their reputation, material wealth or security. In turn, this requires them to find, within themselves, a new fearlessness with which to throw themselves into the overlap; to discover a kindness and compassion to work with the inherent flaws they and others possess. This writing begins to explore some of the practices that sustain those who work in the overlap.

## CHALLENGING THE STATUS QUO

We are ushered into the boardroom, it is large - filled by an imposing oval boardroom table and this executive team, dressed in dark suits, white shirts and bright ties, take most of the seats. They are in twos and threes, deep in conversation about the last topic, I assume. Some of them look up as we enter the room, give us a moment of their attention and return to their conversations.

The CEO has been called away to an important call - we wait for his return. When it comes, he is still barking into his phone, catches sight of us and flashes us one of the loveliest smiles I can recall receiving. My body is confused, though, as it doesn't leave me feeling warm on the inside. He continues his phone conversation and we take in the rest of the room again, nobody else in the team attempts to step forward. Nobody offers to help us settle ourselves or check if we need anything for our presentation. Since the CEO's re-entry, the noise in the room has abated and there are wary looks on most of the faces. I evaluate my psychological response and now feel the way I do when I feel unsafe.

Finally, we begin our agenda item, we are there in response to a request to support the cultural development of this business and have come to the organization via referral. Despite many attempts to make contact in advance of the meeting we have been politely, but repeatedly, refused any chance to talk to the CEO to find out what he wanted from this work. However, now he is full of opinions, almost always voiced in opposition to a statement from us, or one of his team. The ground is decidedly unstable; would you risk putting forward a point of view knowing that it is almost immediately going to dismissed?

One person in particular, however, seems to do well amid this uncertainty. The COO has an air of confidence; she seems to have an uncanny ability to know the 'right' thing to say, when to say it and to whom. In the general air of persecution, she picks her victims accurately, identifying them via the disguised aggression from the CEO, sometimes targeting an idea, sometimes another element of the business and, most devastatingly and regularly, one of her colleagues.

We stutter our way through the agenda item, afraid and far from our best. My stomach feels like it is cramping and it is hard to get the air I need into my lungs. We hesitate before many of our contributions, it is difficult to raise our eyes and connect with the other people in the room and there is no response to any lighter, less serious moments that poke their heads above the parapet.

After a while, we gently offer the first of a couple of honest observations about the effect of this executive team on the rest of the business. Unsurprisingly, it is met with dismissal but we hold firm and now the whole team has a focus for persecution.

There is palpable relief in the room as almost everyone joins in, able to unite as a team in the face of this external intrusion. And yet, as we are escorted out of the building, and in the emails and calls that follow later, we are repeatedly told, in private, that the opinions we offered had a lot of validity and pinpointed the root cause of what was holding back the business.

It isn't easy to challenge the status quo in organizational life, mainly because whatever people might say about their desire for it, the systems we work in have, over many decades, established their own stable patterns. There has often been a convergence of views to a place that is perceived to be least risky; even choices that are about doing something different are usually about a narrow choice between broadly similar options and protests are perceived as subversion. The pressure to survive causes a rejection of any views that don't conform to the dominant perspective.

It is quite a double bind in which we find ourselves. How will we be creative, courageous, intelligent, kind and, at the same time, take no risk? How will we step out and, at the same time, protect ourselves from injury, shame or embarrassment? We often place limits on ourselves, based on our past experiences, that are about our own historical neuroses, not only about the feared response from those we are challenging today.

## THE OLD HEROES

We are sitting in the boardroom two years after the previous CEO resigned, wondering what has happened to this once- great-and-dominant organization. It is all too easy to make simple comparisons between the last regime and this one that paints the old days as the halcyon time when everything was going in the right direction. The current CEO and board members are some of the best people I have worked with, yet their stewardship of the business has been one long period of decline in sales, profits and share price; none of the graphs make enjoyable reading.

I remember what it was like when the previous CEO was there and had a little experience of working with him. It didn't last long and we parted ways amicably enough; he was dubious about the value of our work, I was left bemused by the mismatch between the leader to whom I spoke and the share price plaudits he was receiving.

He had joined because the business needed something of a fresh start; sports- and adrenaline-loving, happy to swear and shout in meetings, with a forensic eye for detail and numbers, he would remember every number and every line of any document flashed in front of him. He ran a board, but to all intents and purposes, was the CEO, the chief financial officer (CFO), the HR director and the COO. That was just for starters.

He bounced. I'm not using this as a metaphor – he literally bounced up to me as we said hello for the first time. He had been appointed to lead the highest-profile division of the group and came with a glorious CV demonstrating success over the past twenty years plus a big smile, shiny teeth, highly-polished shoes and a crisply-ironed button-down shirt.

We spent a couple of hours together and, as I walked away, I had little idea who he was behind the delightful exterior. There are some words that were used over and over again; "fantastic" was the most repeated. As he stood with his hands on his hips, he moved from foot-to-foot, light on the balls of his feet like a tennis player preparing to face a serve. He had one focus, profitability – hitting his numbers and improving the share price; if this could be linked directly to his brilliance as a CEO, then all the better.

For the subsequent two years, the business hit profit targets every quarter and the share price almost doubled. This was achieved by an intense focus on costs: in many places halving the headcount for a particular business unit. Any requests for outside consultants had to be personally-approved by him;

employees were all ranked on performance, their bonuses reduced and the bottom 10% removed each year; members of the top two management tiers were analyzed individually by a recruitment organization and ranked.

Any time figures in the business fell below expectation he addressed them immediately with public remonstrations and shaming, followed by quick and deep cost cuts to get the business back on track. You get the idea. He revelled in his reputation as the alpha male who stood no nonsense, started work at 5am (after a gym workout) and was constantly on an aeroplane. When he was called in to review a business he wanted people to tremble. And they did, usually after spending many days preparing, checking and testing their work to within an inch of its life.

There are different versions of this CEO hero; cumulatively, despite lots of movement and dynamism, they are stuck. Despite everything being 'fantastic' they are struggling to bring difference and energy to the organizations for which they are responsible. And left to their own devices, they will manage their businesses' decline over the next twenty years, retire wealthy and not know what more they could have done to make a difference.

I sound critical but I'm not. Every business needs to be efficient and many allow their costs to run away with them in times of success. The only thing that went wrong here was hard to spot at the time because of the euphoria in the share price. The problem was that the organization was efficient and dying. There were no pockets of life anywhere, the creative juice of the place had gone to sleep or walked out of the door. This was now a place where the internal systems were antiquated and riddled with fragility; the morale of those who were left was down in the dumps; those who had an option elsewhere took it; over time there was a realisation that new ideas had little currency unless they were to do with driving costs down further; there were no competitive new products to match the advances being made by others in the market and the business was losing ground in the newer high-growth markets.

The problem for us in this Age of Connection is to see and then call this out early enough. If we continue running our organizations as highly-efficient machines, they will die, some of them slower than others but they will go. There have to be some conversations in the middle of the euphoria that comes with the benefits of cost-cutting about the next difficult disorientating stage and then the creation of new life at the margins of the current business.

- Where are the conversations about endings, transition and new beginnings taking place?
- How can you identify and amplify them?
- What is the effect of extreme efficiency on the life of your organization?
- Where might you slow down on the efficiency a little to give the new sources of life a chance?
- What, where and how are you experimenting with the new?
- How much attention are the following three phases given in your leadership team meetings and in your organizational communication: ending, disorientation and beginning
- How are you developing your leadership pipeline so that you can live in all three phases simultaneously?

## THE NEO HEROES

They are tired, in a different kind of way to the tiredness of the hero. It is a weary, bone-deep, tiredness. It is not about the miles they have travelled, or the weight they have lifted, the creases in their weary smiles suggest something else. In order to lead, they have had to risk their emotions, their psychological well-being, it is a tiredness that comes more from being vulnerable than from being strong.

I look at them with great pride, they are our heros but not the traditional hero of stories (of business and life), in which an individual goes out into the wilderness to find a foe much stronger than themselves, uses their strength and ingenuity to overcome the odds and returns to a hero's welcome; someone bright, shiny and, above all, superior to the common man; someone in whom we can put our faith, in whom we believe to keep us safe and well; a person on whom we can become dependent.

These new heroes suggest a new myth, one that is as much about their flaws as their perfection. They succeed because of their willingness to keep putting one foot in front of the other, despite the disappointments they repeatedly experience in their leaders, in their organizations, in their peers and often in themselves.

This group of seven sits and contemplates its future. Members have failed to keep their organization from being acquired, failed to protect the livelihoods of the thousands that follow them and failed to make a case for any more time from their parent group. And yet they are the 'Flawed but Willing' to whom this writing is dedicated. These leaders can touch defeat and allow it to play a part in the reality of organizational life. They understand the new myth is one of almost constant mess, dirt, confusion, and iteration, yet somehow they are still described and experienced as elegant - moving with grace. And their teams would put lives in their hands if ever it were required.

Organizations, analysts and the business press talk about these populations in very different ways. They have little exposure to the second group, described above, because there isn't much of a story to tell. This group remains mostly anonymous, mostly committed and when they leave they mostly do so quietly. They are a collective representation of the tens of thousands of people they lead, all the good, all the bad… and all the indifferent.

The first individual is much more familiar. He benefits from a range of biases that reinforce the story about the brilliant strategic individual that led the business to success or to its downfall. They are written about extensively and little consideration is given to the range of forces outside their control or the unintended consequences of many of their choices. There is a vivid match between the leaders' desire to be idealized and everyone else's need to have someone to idealize. A potent alchemy is created, one that is very difficult to break down. After the idealization there is often disappointment in equal measure.

As a whole, maybe our Flawed but Willing theory represents a new myth – that there is no happy ending. There are just beginnings, middles and endings that we collectively plod through, doing our best for those we represent.

It is less dramatic, I know, but maybe we could do with a little less idealization and a little more day-to-day, slightly dull reality. The hardest part of all of this seems to be an acceptance that the central task of leadership as we transition to the Age of Connection may not be to make things better. It may be to allow things to get worse for a while. (See Figure 7)

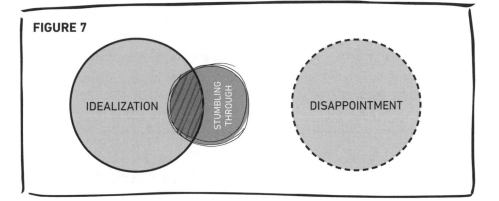

**FIGURE 7**

IDEALIZATION • STUMBLING THROUGH • DISAPPOINTMENT

## RED, HOT AND AGITATED

He is a big man; at a guess, he is not far off retirement and not used to finding himself in this position. His face has turned bright red, contrasting with his shock of grey hair and pink shirt. We are standing together in the middle of the room and the rest of his team, peer group and manager are listening to our conversation. We keep pushing gently into the conversation, he is saying some things about the old business that have needed saying for a while but it is very difficult to stay with the thread of the discussion. There are a number of attempts from his teammates to relieve the discomfort he clearly feels, suggestions for alternative ways of seeing the situation, requests to change the topic, proclamations that enough has been heard, and early attempts at forming a conclusion.

It is easy to understand why this rescuing behaviour is happening, our subject is red, hot, agitated, somehow simultaneously saying "yes" and saying "no" to our discussion. I keep checking with him that he is ok to carry on and, despite the encouragement from his colleagues to stop, and after a brief moment of hesitation, he always says he wants to keep going. I thank him and we hold it together. After a while, at the point of greatest discomfort, without making anything easier or better, we cross a threshold and the room breathes a sigh of relief, we are into new territory and the conversation in the whole room has a more creative feel to it.

There are many of our Flawed but Willing leaders in organizations who are keen to do this work but they need some help to welcome and amplify the point at which they are at their most uncomfortable. This is a key part of our efforts in building our channel at the edge of the status quo: look to make the situation worse, exaggerate and amplify the cause of disturbance and then look for the feedback that accompanies a response. (See figure 8)

- Where might your business need to focus on a point of discomfort for much longer than it is currently doing?
- What are your mechanisms for avoidance, rescuing, tidying up, making better?
- How might you extend the moments of discomfort and agitation?
- How do you feel, personally, about making things worse? What are the triggers and difficulties with which it presents you from your historic habits and ways of being?
- What is the worst you have been?
- What happened in you? What happened around you?

I don't underestimate the difficulty of this work. Over the years, I have come to see a connection between the need to

allow things to get worse and the leadership required to progress through what appear to be irresolvable contradictions
or paradoxes.

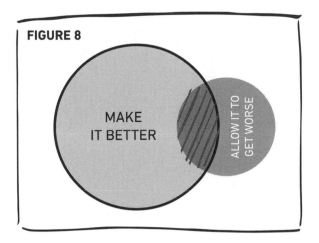

**FIGURE 8**

MAKE
IT BETTER

ALLOW IT TO
GET WORSE

# FIVE

## Love and Power

I was particularly struck with the notion of power and love; in my view both so important in life. I am guessing that some people genuinely have love, some want to love but don't know how. Others don't have it and are honest about that, so at least you know the deal in working for them. The scenario that is worrying me the most is the ones that don't have love but pretend they do - you are fooled for a while then the inconsistencies appear, only small things, but this creates doubt which I think eventually leads to the notion of feeling cheated or let down and finally lack of trust.

This chapter, where you describe your discomfort at a development week, helped me a lot - - because your recoil at the 'inviting and honouring' reassured me that my incipient discomfort about parts of the first couple of chapters - when I encountered what seemed like a bit much 'kind/ gentle/compassionate' and worried things were going a tad dark and soppy - was unjustified. Now I can see the writer doesn't suffer soppy gladly.

## NEGATION OF THE NEGATION

We are in one of those old-fashioned lecture theatres in a university in central London. There is row-upon-row of eager faces, each row slightly elevated over the one in front in a steep bank, all facing the same way towards a speaker at the front of the room. I haven't sat anywhere like this for more than 20 years since I was at university.

Back then, I was bored and unable to see through the dense communication on chemistry and pharmacology in which I was being educated. I was a lost cause, that showed in the fact that I just scraped a qualification and inevitably found myself more drawn to the social, than academic, side of university life. Today though, my attention has been gripped by a lecture, a form of education in which I had lost faith a long time ago.

Course tutor and scriptwriter Robert McKee stood over his lectern, slightly hunched, a face worn with lines and a scowl that kept the most disruptive of his student audience as quiet as church mice. He dared you to be disinterested. Over four long days he talked at us with no interaction required or expected until the breaks hit us. At this point, rather than flood the world with speech, we mostly ended up reflecting and processing a fraction of what had been thrown out to us.

I was there with my father-in-law to learn about screenwriting.

On the third day, McKee hit us with his concept of the 'negation of the negation', something he felt was at the heart of the screenplays that reached inside us and helped us feel the painful reality of the world. The plot twists and turns would not simply move from one pole to the other and back again, that was the stuff of simple fairy tales. From good to bad and back again; from love to hate and back again; or from joy to sorrow and back again. The 'negation of the negation' was a dramatic vehicle that posed an irresolvable dilemma. The example that hit me hardest on a personal level was the plot at the heart of a film called Ordinary People released in 1980 and directed by Robert Redford.

The relationship between the character of the youngest son and his mother was predicated on the societal expectation, (and presented image), of love, while the reality of the experience felt more like hatred - especially in contrast to the relationship between his mother and older brother. It represented the 'negation of the negation' - to be hated while being told that you are loved; to be hated while it looks, to the rest of the world, as if you are being loved.

What a powerful and terrible position in which to be put, knowing whichever way you turn is unpalatable at best, life-destroying at worst: In this case, having to accept your mother hates you or living a lie and pretending to yourself and others that she loves you.

## MAMMA MIA

I am sitting looking through my phone lens, pretending to take a video of my two children and their two friends dancing maniacally to ABBA's Mamma Mia. They range in age from three to seven years-old, throwing their hands around, shaking their heads, periodically jumping, and taking up the space in the room. This has emerged without a plan or an announcement that it was going to happen. I am struggling. What makes this scene a little more unusual is that three of the four parents in this scene have also started dancing - my wife and her two friends. It is just after lunchtime, there is no alcohol involved and I am frozen. "Come on daddy!" says my eldest. I am paralyzed by what I imagine is a double bind, an irresolvable dilemma.

I know all about the theory of spontaneity and precisely what it is in my psychological development that fears it, I have worked hard in the professional setting for this not to be a problem and now, I realise, caught truly off-guard, how little progress I have made. "Be spontaneous" is the internal command. And yet, the harder I try, the further I am from being spontaneous and the phonier I feel when I have a go. If I don't try, I feel defeated by my inability to let go and join in. So though it is better to stay stuck in the contradiction, this place is also full of anxiety. I smile and grimace my way through the song, relieved that, in the 1970s, singles tended to last less than four minutes and that the dancing spontaneously moves onto something else afterwards.

I think the two conflicting messages in my head were something like 'be spontaneous and creative' combined with 'don't look silly. It's shameful to lose control'.

## WHAT IS THE WAY THROUGH THESE DOUBLE BINDS?

This concept of 'double binds', or irresolvable dilemmas, is at the heart of the challenge our large organizations are now facing. The irresolvable dilemma at the heart of the transition is our Flawed but Willing in environments where they are asked to be creative and yet take no risk.

I have an instinct that the double binds are here as a key part of the transition from one age to the next. They are here to teach us something and give us something as we experience them. They are here because, without them, it wouldn't be a phase shift; it would just be an incremental step from one place to the next.

If you are going to make it through this transition where you encourage things to get worse and not only better; where you are stumbling through and are not easy to idealize; where the in-between phase is anxiety-provoking, disorientating and ambiguous, I suggest you need a rare integration of power and love to see you through.

## ABUSIVE OR ANAEMIC?

Why do I put myself through these 'development weeks'? They are always full of well-meaning and warm individuals who are struggling to make their work relevant to the rest of us. Yet I keep coming back because there is usually a nugget or two that shifts my understanding of, or insight into, the world of work fundamentally. But this time, two days in, I'm starting to doubt my own sanity; many of the rest of the participants have been together before so immediately they have their shared experience and language to fall back on. There is lots of 'inviting' each other to do things and 'honouring' of each other's experience. Aaaargh! If one more person invites or honours me I will explode.

At its worst, this gathering feels like one of those 1970s cults I have read about but was too young to experience, they have their own spiritual leader, a text that is revered and a community of followers most of whom seem to have lost their ability to discern and challenge what is being presented to them. Why would they? Everything is a gift isn't it? Am I the only one chuckling to myself as I get fed up and say this to the group? No-one else even smiles and there is a struggle to keep on loving me when I steadfastly refuse to be touched.

Subsequently, there isn't a lot more 'inviting' for me and I am left to my own devices, with my grumpiness. I keep going to the classes, but am in half a mind to book an early flight home to my family. I'm glad I stayed; on the Wednesday night we start talking about the importance of power to counter-balance the importance of love if we are to change stuck societies and businesses.

The lecture room is packed, considering this is an optional session after dinner on the Wednesday evening. I was surprised to hear the audience noise as I opened the door and peered at a sea of 'backs of heads' as I looked for a seat. I would have preferred a seat that allowed for a quick exit if needed, but I had no such luck and found myself ushered to one half-way down the room, on the far left, with only one exit point to the row.

There are eleven pairs of knees between me and my escape route. We settle down and I keep my coat on, defiantly - my signals have never been subtle. I am quick to give in, however, and the layers of clothing start coming off as the presentation and conversation pique my interest.

There is a particular section in which a quote attributed to Martin Luther King is offered up. I hadn't heard it before, it nailed it, and finally I had some justification for my righteousness.

"You see, what happened is that some of our philosophers got off base. And one of the great problems of history is that the concepts of love and power have usually been contrasted as opposites, polar opposites, so that love is identified with a resignation of power, and power with a denial of love. It was this misinterpretation that caused the philosopher Nietzsche, who was a philosopher of the will to power, to reject the Christian concept of love. It was this same misinterpretation, which induced Christian theologians to reject Nietzsche's philosophy of the will to power in the name of the Christian idea of love. Now, we got to get this thing right. What is needed is a realization that power without love is reckless and abusive, and that love without power is sentimental and anaemic."

*King, Martin Luther Jr. 1967* [5]

This was delivered with impact to an audience clinging hard to the notion that love is the only way through anything with which we are confronted. They have grown up, as I have, in a series of Industrial Age institutions. We have been encouraged to believe in cultures ruled by patriarchs who manifest their power through domination and submission. Personal drive and stamina win the day, we have been taught to believe in a world of leaders and followers, the most powerful moving to the top of the heap, the rest of us knocked down, accepting a belief that only the losers, the weak and inept allow themselves to be pushed aside, to be marginalized.

How should we respond when faced with this problem?

With an overwhelming emphasis on love as a polar opposite to the form of power from which we have suffered. But love without power is sentimental and anaemic. (See figure 9)

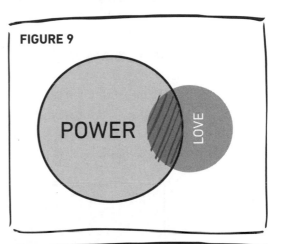

**FIGURE 9**

That is not to say love isn't needed and magical, we just have to find a way in which both these forces can be integrated if we are to find our way though to the next age. So, in building our channel, we want to strengthen it with both power and love, (or

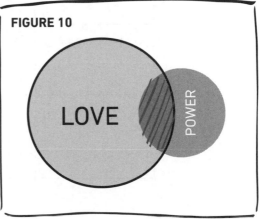

**FIGURE 10**

with whichever words mean something to you and illustrate these concepts). (See figure 10)

This integration is a different kind of consciousness than exists, at present, in most large organizations and most communities of change agents.

I have used the concepts of love and power to structure the following section of the book. Looking at mindsets, feelings and behaviours that can strengthen us to be 'fearless and unwavering as an expression of power; to be aware and gentle as an expression of love'.

There is no attempt to define a formula here (or 'six steps to heaven'). It is just a structure that will do for now and may serve no other purpose than to make the navigation of this book a little easier.

| Valiance | The courage to dance on the edge of tolerance - one foot inside, one foot outside of, the established order . To overcome the fear of being shunned or thought irrelevant |
| --- | --- |
| Gentleness | To be able to retain an open heart, despite the defensive closed postures of others. Caring for all the people you work with, not only those who like you |
| Awareness | An intelligence that is not solely intellectual, emotional or spiritual but is, in fact, a kind of collective awareness. One that doesn't know, can't predict but can sense, moment-by-moment, and respond |

| Persistence | To stand firm, when not comprehending how to cope; to lament and accept losses and defeats along the way while not giving up on the ultimate intention |
| --- | --- |

Each capability also breaks down into three sub-sections, outlining practices that may help develop the capability.

**'Inside myself' practices.** Working on the intra-personal level, what is the work to be done on my own ways of being, thinking and acting?

**'Between us both' practices.** Working on the inter-personal level on the relationships between myself and others.

**'Across us all' practices.** Working on something beyond the inter-personal. The spirit that connects us all in an organization above and beyond our individual relationships. Those that have been here before us can inform practices, as much as can those with whom we currently work.

# SIX

## Valiance

The connection of anger and fear is
brilliant. It has set off a myriad of
thoughts in me but the key thought is that
this is a central issue at the top table. I
like the point on "anger" being admired or
the stuff of myths in the Industrial Age.
And indeed now in organizations: "strong
leader, courageous conversations, cuts
through the crap" etc. all labels I hear
around our organization! And what you set
out beautifully is that for you, and I know
for many of the "angry leaders" fear is
their real emotion, which they are not able
to voice.

I love your stories. You tell them beautifully,
they draw me in, and there is always an
element of the unexpected. I read them avidly,
wanting to know where they will lead. Both
you and all the other characters display their
vulnerability and uncertainty, even though in
the main those featured are successful and
acknowledged to be so, in one way or another.

# SIX (A)

## Practices for inside myself

### BEAUTIFUL MINDS AND SCRUFFY SUITS

They pride themselves on their cool, rational thought and their training that means they are relied upon by the rest of the organization to underpin the financial heart of the place. Many of them have an actuarial training and their business of insurance relies on the elegant calculations they perform. I have enjoyed getting to know them over the past few months, they are prickly to begin with, and very closed to anything I may have to offer. Over time, they give more of themselves and I realize, with a thump, how little people listen to them, beyond issues relating to their core competence. It is a strange divide; on their subject of expertise their voices are loud and their opinions well-received and respected. On most other matters, they are politely ignored, as if they can't possibly understand the other workings of the organization.

We are talking together because they are having difficulty applying the same perfect logic they bring to their analysis to themselves. The department is being restructured by a new leader, the evidence has been gathered, the inputs offered, interpretations completed and yet the conclusions are peculiar. The room is a collection of highly-intelligent individuals, so fascinated by their minds they have forgotten about the rest of their bodies. I note a range of spectacles, unkempt hairstyles and suits that say "just give me something to wear that I don't have to think about each day". There are a number of awkward monologues and courteous, 'bi-polar' disagreements which leave the opposing party feeling well-liked and dismissed.

Over time, we come to agree there is something amiss in what they are suggesting for their own department. They tend to favour current practice over the best-available evidence. They are following what their peer group is doing, even when it has been demonstrated not to work. They behave as if doing more of what they do is the same as doing what they do more effectively. They focus on surface symptoms rather than root causes. The most devastating realization for them is that they are failing to present information or choices effectively. They have been trained to remove bias and yet here is bias in spades and bucket loads.

This team makes a useful example precisely because of its training, but the situation is a common one. It is hard to let go of what we know and what we are, for what we could become. The other reason this team stays with me is that members were able to do what many others couldn't, which was to describe how frightening it was to let go of past biases.

We worked on some practices together that were designed to help us experience our organizational lives more directly, practices that put them in the overlap, opening the choice between static or dynamic, fearful or fearless. I need to find a better word than fearless because the actual manifestation of their being was still fearful and yet moving. (See Figure 11)

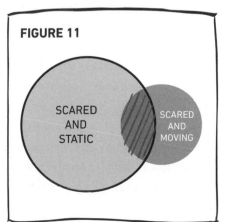

**FIGURE 11**

SCARED AND STATIC

SCARED AND MOVING

## ANGER OVER FEAR

At first, I felt very angry, they were having a go at me, my whole body was flushed with an enormous surge of emotion. My mind was trying to grab anything that would get me through this and everything in my body was ready for a fight.

Then I stopped and gave it a little longer. It may only have been seconds, but felt much longer, as these things often do.

Now I noticed a sensation in my stomach that is difficult to describe but I knew it, after many years of experience, to be a sign that I was scared. My intestines were all tangled up, I was hyper-sensitive to the environment and my heart was in my mouth. I used to deny this being about fear and call it something else; I couldn't accept I would be scared of anything, far better to be angry than scared.

Now I can accept it is fear, it gives me some more choices.

I also know that, when I feel it, there is bound to be some anger somewhere, sometimes directed towards me. This is helpful when everyone in the room is still smiling but my senses are telling me something different. Sometimes, it is more 'obvious', people avoiding contact with me, talking past me and turning their faces away.

It is then a choice of what do I do with this? Do I want to press into the anger, encourage its expression? I often do this by reflecting back to the team their facial expressions - this sometimes causes a shift. Or do I want to diffuse the anger? In this case I chose to do that in the interests of the bigger piece of work by trying an apology. But I could only make this choice once I distinguished fear as different to anger. If I only had an angry response there was no choice about my reactions.

I imagine a picture of my fear when it is hiding just behind my anger. It is smaller, obscured somehow, it makes itself available but only for an instant before it hides away again, hands over its eyes or ears or mouth. If I can pause and wait quietly then it may show itself again. The fearful part of me feels weak but the more I wait, the more time I give it, the more likely it is that it will come and speak for itself.

When I speak from that place, I notice the whole tone of what I am saying changes, my voice and presence are different, steadier more connected, the audience is more intent on hearing what I have to say, the room is quieter. And we get a result more often than not.

In the Establishment, it is quite easy to be angry with a whole host of things in the business that are not going to plan. In the culture of the Industrial Age, being angry is often admired as a form of leadership and if it is not admired, then it is certainly the currency of many organizational myths.

In the channel at the edges of the status quo, access to fear, especially the fear behind any anger, is a source of creativity and change, if only we can give it a voice. (See Figure 12)

**FIGURE 12**

ANGER  FEAR

- Where does anger arise most often in your system? And when?
- Can you identify what triggers it?
- Is it authentic, about addressing some kind of injustice?
- Is it a cover for another emotion?
- Could you be covering up fear?
- If so, what are you scared of? Can you articulate it or write it down? What happens? How do people react?
- Can you distinguish the changes in your body and the distinctions between what you notice when you are angry, compared with when you are scared?

## SHALLOW BREATHING

We walk into a new section of the building, my footfall is definitely less heavy here, something has changed in the thickness of the floor covering. It is quiet here too, as if we have closed the door on the real world of this business and entered hallowed ground.

The two people we are here to meet are buttoned up, the clothing is all very 'on-trend' and I feel slightly intimidated, the way I do when entering a luxury retail store. They are leading the CEO's strategy group. As far as I understand, it is a kind of skunkworks set up to handle strategic breakthroughs and we are talking to them because they are a little stuck.

Their smiles are cold and we begin with a time check. We have sixty minutes, but they need to be away in 45, important business for the CEO. There are regular time checks every ten minutes from one or the other checking on our progress and I am more than a little pissed off before the second one.

There is no space to breathe here; it is a parallel of the environment they have set up for this strategy group. They hand-select high-potential individuals from the global business and bring them to the corporate headquarters for a 12-month stint. They are tasked with making a breakthrough on some issue of strategy that a local business unit has dragged its heels on. After doing the 'thinking', they hand it back to the business unit and, hopefully, as a result of their increased profile and access to the CEO, go on to an immediate promotion back in their country.

The team was run by the two people I was meeting, one was the leader, the other an internal process consultant with a specialism in six sigma approaches. They coached the selected few during their time in the corporate headquarters. As I was already experiencing, there was a significant emphasis on process and structure and being neat, ordered, smart.

The problem was, they were having no breakthroughs. Even those they claimed to have had looked good on paper but didn't stand up to much scrutiny. Few breakthroughs were sustained - partly because the local business resented being given an answer to implement, partly because there was no space for creativity, diversity, disturbance or difference. And it all showed up in the conversation. I call it a conversation, it was more of an examination. They were looking for quick, easy answers and weren't too keen on a world view that challenged their own highly-developed perception.

Most of all, there was no room for anything outside of their prescribed process. As we were escorted back over the perimeter I noticed my chest expand a little and let out a couple of deep sighs before I felt 'back in my body' again. You won't be surprised to hear this was another of my not-so-glorious failures and we weren't invited back for another conversation.

When we are scared or in an environment that is scared, we forget to breathe. Or, at least, forget to breathe so that the breath goes all the way into our bodies and nourishes us. It often gets stuck in the upper chest, quickly moving in and out in a shallow manner. So it is a simple practice but one that has immense power when you are scared and in the container.

- When you are scared, how do you breathe?
- When does your chest feel tight, physically or metaphorically?
- What are the signals and symptoms of suffocation in the organization?
- Learn to take some sighs and deep breaths so that they reach the cavities in your body. I don't mean hyperventilating
- As you learn to breathe what do you notice in your body and mind? What happens to your fear?

## BEING DIFFERENT

It was a strange charade in which I took part every Monday morning in the workplace. The 'real men' I aspired to be like had played rugby or watched rugby over the weekend. The White, middle-class population that made up this corporation shared their real-or-metaphorical bruises on a Monday morning and laughed with each other. It seemed to set up an easier working relationship for the rest of the week.

I wasn't White or middle-class and had no interest in rugby, but somehow I forced myself into sounding and looking the same so I could fit in. I could give you a dozen other examples of how I bent myself to fit in for the first 10 years of my career. The most damaging was when I was suffering at the hands of bullies and only realise now that they got away with it because I was so desperate to be like them, to please the image I had of a senior executive in this organization and fit in.

The ultimate irony was that, as the years progressed and diversity in the workplace became a fashionable focus for organizations, I was repeatedly used as a representation of diversity at a senior level. "We can't be prejudiced," went the argument – "otherwise he wouldn't be a director." I had a rude awakening when confronted by one of my junior colleagues on this issue.

"You may be the poster child for diversity around here but you are just as White middle-class and male on the inside as the rest of them. You just look different on the outside. That isn't the kind of diversity we are meant to be talking about."

I denied many aspects of myself in order to make this pretence work. My initial education, where I had started my career, my accent, a degree I didn't want to do, how much I loved the people side of things, how wrong I believed many of our management practices were, what I liked, what I knew about and pretended not to.

I convinced myself that the organization wanted my energy and commitment but not my difference. Looking back on it now, I wonder if the responsibility for this farce was 50:50 theirs and mine. I look back now and wonder how much the many talented people around me were denying of themselves; what more we could have gained if we had enjoyed our individual weirdness instead.

Those who had the courage to be their different selves and were not rejected seemed to be treated as a novelty. They were accepted for the value they brought, but limited in how far they might progress in the organization or with what they would be trusted. Our recruitment processes also unconsciously reinforced the need to be the same, rooting out difference even when the brief was specifically to find it.

Fortunately, I realised later on – and not too late – that I wanted to celebrate my difference, not hide it. It took a while, and was initially motivated by giving up on what anyone else might think or say; internally, I was daring them to sack me but something unexpected happened. I became more successful and the promotions followed more quickly until eventually I ran the place. I do my best now to make not fitting in a badge of honour rather than a reason for removal. We celebrate individual weirdness, encourage people to talk about it, and there has been an interesting, unintended consequence. Giving up the desire to fit in means the energy that the bullies feed on is removed, their power is diminished.

Giving up the desire to fit into the current culture helps build and strengthen the shift between the Industrial Age and the Age of Connection. If you are serious about the phase shift to a new age then looking for, and amplifying, your difference and the difference in others is a key part of the process.

A risk of standing out is that you may have to give up your desire for progress in promotional terms. Or it may accelerate you. You won't know until you try. (See Figure 13)

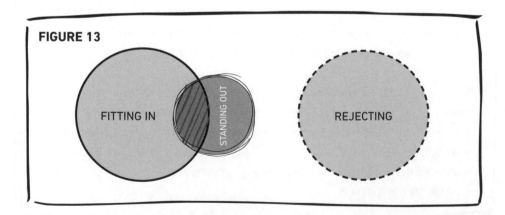

**FIGURE 13**

FITTING IN

STANDING OUT

REJECTING

- Where do you fit? Where do you stand out?
- What is weird about you? According to the current paradigm, what do you reject? What do you deny?
- What does your difference represent? What could you symbolize for the future?
- How can you make your difference useful to yourself and the organization? Where is it accepted and denied? Where will you do something new? Why can't it be accepted? What would have to be given up by the status quo? Where are you agreeing in order to fit in?

## THE ARTIST'S BIN

It was hard to imagine the business structure without his team there, their creation was based on the insight of which he was most proud and they couldn't let it go. We had admired his work over the years from a distance – he was one of those that the original Challenger research was based on. He is a little older now, a little greyer around the temples, a little more conservative in his dress, a little slower with his speech. Eventually, I recognise what the tonal difference in our conversation means. He is less certain:

"It struck us a while ago that there was a group of leading-edge customers which was exerting disproportionate influence on the market and yet our sales force was set up mostly to hit as many customers as possible, as many times as possible, with a consistent message across all customer groups,' he says. "Marketing had most of the power in the business so we were organized around brands and 'key messages'. It took a lot of work but I led the effort to change this mindset in the business."

The structure re-organized around customers rather than brands. There had been a lot of investment in time and money and now the data were telling him, after the excitement of the first couple of years, that the model wasn't working as well as hoped. The need for strong brands at the heart of the business model was reasserting itself. It was time for another change that he was fighting to the point of his own health suffering.

We are talking because his health and his performance rating are in jeopardy.

I gather my breath and wonder if there is another way to approach his wellbeing. Much of the work we have already completed has left him no better off. His attachment to something on which he has based his identity is overwhelming any other efforts to help.

"I was told once, on a writing course, to identify the most beautiful line in a paragraph or chapter or book and discard it," I say. "The idea was that I would be so attached to the beauty I would end up forcing other parts to fit and the result would be clumsy or uncomfortable".

He is lost in thought for a while and then turns his face back to me.

"I actually do that too quite often when I'm writing papers, believe it or not, because you do get hung up on a sentence or an opening. Exactly the same thing happens when I am painting, there's a piece of it that took considerable crafting but as the painting evolves it increasingly doesn't fit and finally you paint over it."

Building our channel at the edges of the Establishment – we need some artistry, the ability to create something highly personal and yet throw it away easily, this is going to help the next phase emerge. The courage to let go of something we may strongly believe, in order to allow something else to emerge. (See figure 14)

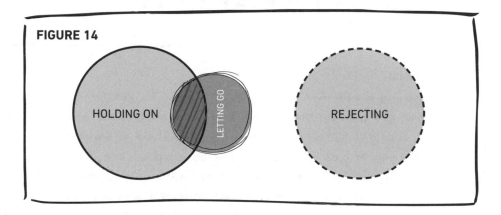

**FIGURE 14**

HOLDING ON — LETTING GO — REJECTING

- What is it in the organizational view to which you are most attached or are most likely to reject?
- What effect is it having on you?
- What effect is it having on everything else around it?
- Where do you have to force things?
- What if you took your most 'beautiful line' and threw it away?
- What if you took the line to which you were most averse and kept to it?

# SIX (B)

## Practices for between us

### WILD MAN

He is usually a mild-mannered man, known for his gentle demeanor and care for others. His smile is almost never absent from his face and his efforts are always on behalf of someone else. An email or call is never going to be a selfish one, he will be contacting you to try to help someone, make connections, offer his services. We have known each other for a number of years but this is the first time he has asked for help for himself. This time he couldn't make it work with what he had, the winning formula had run out of steam and he was lost.

More than his being lost, I was most concerned by his lack of a smile when we greeted each other; his mop of hair, round face and glasses, framed by a painful circular frown, arching over dark-brown eyes. His back was aching - it wouldn't let him sit down for long - so his story was interspersed with slow movements up from the chair, a walk around the room and then a slow lowering back into his seat. He was struggling with a boss who couldn't be satisfied, no matter how much he tried to do, what had always worked in the past.

"I felt he was complaining and how unfair the accusations were, it was unrelenting aggression and I couldn't escape from it. I just listened quietly after trying a couple of times to put my point across."

"What would you like to do to him?" I asked after a particularly long story of suffering. There was then another ten minutes of explanation that it wasn't really his manager's fault and outlining all the extenuating circumstances.

"Yes but what would you like to do in your most wild state?"

"I would like to knock his block off," he says, with his hands shaping up to circle something.

"That looks more like a strangling motion than a punching one." He laughs out loud, looking at his hands.

"Yes. Ok then, I'd strangle him."

"Go on, have a go, pretend that is his neck you have in your hands." That was too much, he is embarrassed and looks down, puts his hands away.

I apologize. "Sorry, I should have said none of this is intended to hurt anyone. My hypothesis is that you have a wild part of your nature that doesn't get enough expression. It is causing you difficulty with your energy and your physical symptoms."

He is slumped on the desk, hands over his ears, elbows on the table, energy drained from his body, but makes a strong connection with the suggestion. I sense the slump is an expression of how he feels during some of the interactions he describes.

We worked a lot more with what he wanted to say. It wasn't immediate, but slowly, as he accessed this wild man hidden behind the jovial exterior, the symptoms began to alleviate. We started with journaling, building up to saying it out loud in private and then, on a very emotional day, finding the voice to speak it in person to the offending party. His expression wasn't inappropriate in any way despite accessing some wildness in order to be able to express it.

We have long since given up on our wild nature, being wild is seen as being unprofessional. Instinctively, wild men and women who can't let the wildness out surround us. But the Flawed but Willing know they have to build a channel that can withstand this part of themselves and others. There is a creative use for our wild natures if we can find an expression of it that doesn't hurt others; sometimes the seed of the transition is buried inside a scream.

We can cope with socially-permitted aggression in the Establishment. That is not what I am talking about. That is often just about dumping your stress on others or acting out some psychological need to demean other people around you. Neither am I talking about a wild state of anarchy that characterizes chaos, breakdown and fragmentation. But, at the edges of these states, what is the part of you that just wants to shout out loud at the injustice, limited thinking, avoidance or lack of integrity around the place? That is what we are after. (See Figure 15)

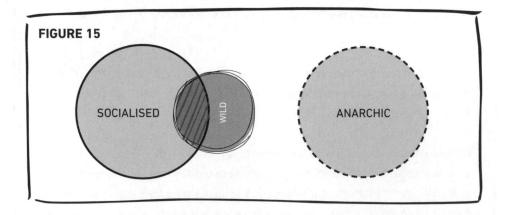

**FIGURE 15**

SOCIALISED     WILD          ANARCHIC

- Are there any archetypes of wild men or women with whom you identify? e.g. woodsman, hunter, criminal, hermit, warrior, wolf woman or herdsman?

- How do you picture the wild man expression of yourself?
- Could you draw or describe the figure?
- How is this version of you kept in check in relationship with others?
- What are the benefits and sacrifices of this mechanism that keeps you in check?
- Where do you want to let him or her out and what would the positive consequences be for you and others?

## SAYING YES

My business partner and I are sitting in the very plush offices of a private equity firm in London, having been invited there by the managing partner, someone my business partner has known for many years. They struck up a strong working relationship through a previous project in another company and he wants to support us in getting our new business off the ground. We are interested in doing the high-end psychologically- and spiritually-based work that will help CEOs and their executive teams prepare their businesses for this uncertain future in the Age of Connection.

I am new to the field, having just left the industrial corporate world to follow my passion and interest. I feel comfortable in this office, I can understand the feel of the place, the language used, the way people move. I fantasize about what is going on in their day and the challenges that cause their brows to be so furrowed. A very smart PA clicks into the meeting room with an important-looking print-out for our prospective client. He excuses himself, pores over it, makes some scribbles, then calls his wife to discuss tiling for their home improvement project.

We have a laugh and a coffee, the two of them reminiscing about old times and then get down to business. The organization has difficulty interviewing prospective businesses and the people in them, with a view to purchasing these and recruiting new management teams, if needed.

"Can we help them with interviewing skills?"

My heart sinks. "What a shame," I think; "We can do so much more than that." (Maybe he doesn't realise quite how special we are. Oh well, we will politely decline and make our way to the next appointment.)

"Yes," says this clear voice sitting next to me.
"We can help with that and do it in a way that you won't have tested before."

I have a quizzical expression on my face and lots of doubt in my head but keep my mouth shut and my head nodding affirmatively. A few minutes later, we have said our goodbyes and are wrapped up against the cold of London in February.

"I have no idea how to do that," I say, wanting to sound curious, but actually sounding reproachful.

"Neither do I",says my business partner, pointing at a bookshop. "But the first thing we are going to do is to buy a couple of books on interviewing skills and work out how to build our work into their principles."

I have mused, in the past, about an experiment that could somehow measure how many times people say "no" in an average day in the Establishment. In my experience, there is an inbuilt fear of saying "yes" to the uncertain. We find it much easier when saying "no" fulfills a need to look clever, to make the person asking the question look worse, to demonstrate the 'quality' of our thinking or to be in opposition.

The channel being built to help the transition to the next age is strengthened by saying "yes". Saying "yes", when you can think of lots of reasons to say "no", is at the heart of experimentation and could access the hidden possibility present in your organization - one you just can't see yet. (See Figure 16)

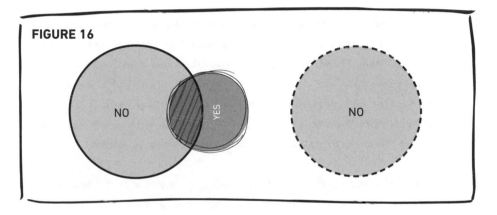

**FIGURE 16**

Experiment with how many times you say "no" to the uncertain in your day or week. Yes, I do literally mean record it somewhere, like a 'symptom diary'.

- Can you see any patterns in what you are saying "no" to?
- What are the conditions around you when it happens?
- Track how energetic you feel and what it does to the energy of those around you.

When you have enough data, try an experiment with saying "yes"; literally spend the whole day saying "yes". (You can always undo them the next day if need be, just give the experiment a whole-hearted go).

- Can you see any patterns emerging as you say "yes" to it all?
- What are the conditions around you when it happens?
- Track how energetic you feel and what it does to the energy of those around you.

## CRACKING OPEN

I hadn't ever been allowed past it, the protective shell around the inner experience that was at the heart of who he was. It was just too strong, the defences were multitudinal and he left me wondering what it was that was so difficult he wouldn't want to access it. Our conversations were pleasant enough, but I doubt I did much more at the start than be someone with which he could talk in confidence to relieve the loneliness once a month.

In addition to the psychological defences, there were others too - forms of self-medicating to keep the anxiety from being 'discovered', excessive work, over control, alcohol and affairs. The defences had served him well in many ways. He was rich, successful, powerful, had reached the position of CEO that had always been the ultimate aim. He was still married, had three beautiful children and a stunning home that his wife had designed and built. And yet, it was just taking too much out of him, he was angry and upset most of the time when at home, over-pleasant and 'adapted' most of the time at work.

Then, one day, we were fortunate with the timing of our conversation (or maybe there are no accidents). Everything had gone wrong at the same time that day - work, home and health. We met at the end of a few hours that had held no respite. The relationship he most treasured with his chairman and mentor had taken a turn for the worse and he had intended, but forgotten, to cancel our conversation.

It was in that moment of finally being overwhelmed that we had a tiny glimpse into the core of his being and about what he what he was most defensive. As we worked on the difficulties of the day and his responses to them, there was a story he told me briefly. It is one that I have been permitted and privileged to hear many times over the years from others - of childhood abuse. Sometimes sexual, often physical and always emotional in some way; experiences of over-intrusion or neglect or both.

His body shuddered and he couldn't stop his hand shaking as he spoke. There was a gentle sigh in us both as we allowed ourselves to talk about the unspeakable for just a few minutes before it had to be put away again.

We drew a diagram together which helped make some more sense of what was going on and took the emotional pitch down a level. It was a way of welcoming the conversation and it not being too much to bear. It felt as if, once we had turned to scribbling our sense-making onto paper, the enormity of what was being shared was easier to talk about.

Being overwhelmed is something of which we are fearful and, at the same time, something that can be helpful as we transition from one age to the next.

If our defences are like a brick wall, always solid, never breached, then the possibility of anything novel emerging is reduced. It often takes a moment of being overwhelmed before the part of us that we are defending can be seen. In the moment of being hurt, overloaded, caught out, tripped up or humiliated we gain a chance to see, and work with, the part of ourselves we spend the rest of our time enclosing in a protective shell.

As we spend time at the edges of the things we know and with which we can cope, the channel is strengthened. When we can't cope, the cracks can allow us to integrate an experience that has been shielded for a lifetime but refuses to vanish or stop causing problems in the rest of our lives. (See Figure 17)

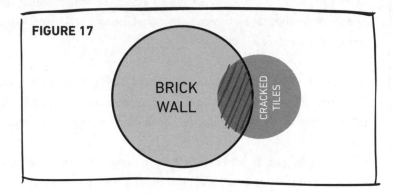

**FIGURE 17**

BRICK WALL

CRACKED TILES

- What are you defending or shielding most strongly in yourself?
- How does this keep you rooted to the status quo?
- What are the defences you are using (psychological, emotional, behavioural and relational - at home and at work)?
- What are the defences designed to stop you from saying, showing or doing?
- What happens to your defences when you are overwhelmed?
- What are the opportunities these moments present to you?
- What is the worst that could happen if you were to expose the inner workings of your weaker, under-developed, more vulnerable self?
- And what is the best that could happen?

## MY INNER PAVAROTTI

There are 14 of us standing in a circle in a small, long, wooden-floored, stark room in Camden, north London. I have a feeling that I haven't experienced for a long time. I feel so exposed and vulnerable, I am fairly sure I am not going to make it to the end of this exercise. I may have to make a feeble excuse, step outside, grab mouthfuls of fresh air and decide if I am going to do a runner.

I knew when my friend Steve sent me the invitation to a day of 'musical improvisation' that it was something I really, really didn't want to do, so of course I hovered over the delete button and then replied to say "yes", I would be there. I trust Steve and have been involved in a range of experiences in theatre in the past but there was something about singing, in particular, that was disturbing me. I thought it was worth trying to find out why.

Back in the room, I found my constrained, corporate self standing in the middle of a group of artistic media types, all converse trainers, crumpled jackets and shirts hanging out. The idea of this exercise is that the piano player plays a tune in a particular style and you sing to it - in gibberish - nothing has to make any sense, but it needs to match the musical style of the accompaniment. The person to your left starts singing to you and you have to respond in some way, again in gibberish. Then, when you have finished, the music changes, you turn to your right and sing to the next person in the new style. So we go around the circle.

I am standing about six people along the line, working out when and how to make my exit. The first few rounds do nothing to quell my panic but it is all happening too quickly and, all of a sudden, there he is, my first partner, completing his piece and turning towards me. We have never met before and have no particular connection. I find myself unable to look at him and am turned away at a slight angle. As my eyes travel around the room, I settle on the facilitator who catches my eye. She has been a caring presence since we began the work and I feel comfortable again for a moment. She makes a slight gesture with her hand, indicating that I should turn my head and look at my partner as he starts to respond to the music... oh, for heaven's sake, it is something operatic!

He starts singing and it takes my breath away, the room goes still. It wasn't that he was any good; frankly, I can't remember whether he was even in tune. The magic was in the degree of commitment he brought to his singing and to me, as his partner. There was no chance he would be half-hearted in his delivery and, despite my obvious discomfort, no chance he would hold back in his interaction with me. I was spellbound.

And then, without warning, he finishes singing. I open my mouth and out comes something I don't recognize, I haven't planned for it and, all-of-a-sudden, have lost my self-consciousness. Again, I can't recall the quality of what I produced, just that it was similarly whole-hearted. At the moment we build to a duet and finish our piece, it seems natural and obvious to give him a heart-felt hug. Two blokes that have never met before, at least one of who is not very tactile at the best of times.

The rest of the day is stimulating and enlightening but nothing else touches that moment. As I reflect back on it in the days and weeks that follow, I know it has done something to my visceral understanding of commitment in a way that is impossible for me to forget or unlearn.

I am left asking myself some questions that are now posed to you.
- Where, when and to whom in my organization am I committed?
- Where do I hold myself back?
- When do I give myself fully?
- And what is the role of commitment in living a successful, creative life?

# SIX (C)

## Practices for across us all

### IMPERFECT CONTRIBUTIONS

The CEO has some key strands to his strategy for the future and one of them contains the word 'empowerment'. He has reasoned that, with the technical advantage of his business being fast eroded, the freedom of his global employees to innovate could be a critical source of advantage in the future.

The project team of 12 colleagues gathered around the meeting table wear pursed lips and severe frowns, these people were responsible for this 'empowerment strategy' and the conversation had been becoming increasingly difficult. They were making little progress and were expecting a visit from the project leader in the next hour.

A few minutes late, in she rushes, a whirlwind of power, and the mood changes in the room - from collective frustration to collective fear and a desire to look good. She listens in to the conversation for ten minutes or so as the team becomes increasingly confused and stilted under her gaze. The discussion sounds familiar to me; those organizations that most need empowered employees have cultures that are least likely to allow those initial faltering steps towards it to take place.

"We can't just let chaos reign in the organization, we have to give people some boundaries."

"Yes, exactly, defined areas within which people are empowered, outside of which they should ask before acting."

"We need to define 'empowerment' more clearly, we can't just leave it as open as it currently is, people are confused."

There are some dissenting voices, mine included, that argue for space and time for the organization to feel its way through this initial period; to generate some imperfect experience from which learning can take place. And then we are hit with the impatience of the Establishment.

"Ok, I've heard enough," says the project leader. "If you can't sort this out despite all the time you have spent on it, I'll have to do it myself."

The difficulty creating an empowered business was highlighted in a sentence. This is what it was like to try and work it out for oneself inside this organization.

She was true to her word and, a couple of hours later, had given the problem to one of the big consulting houses that were supporting the strategy implementation. Back it came in pristine blue and white the next day. A definition of empowerment, two sentences on one slide, each word defined precisely. What it did mean and what it didn't mean. The expression was great, definite, clear, the boundaries everyone had been keen to have. Within 24 hours it had been put under the noses of all relevant stakeholders and was ready to be rolled-out. And rolled-out it was, over and over again... with little effect. You see, in that instant, the signal had been sent and clearly received. There are a few people with big brains at the top of this organization, they do the thinking and then give you some rules to live within. Don't step outside of those; if you do, you will have no excuse as you have been told clearly what the right side of the line is.

The Industrial Age believes it is good at requesting, and often achieving, something close to perfect compliance. The language, metaphors and measures of mechanics and machines has left in us a desire and belief that this is possible if only we lead the right people in the right way (and of course check up on them).

The transition to the Age of Connection will need in us an equally powerful belief and desire for imperfect contribution, which leads to more contribution and sets up a virtuous cycle of energetic belief. It must build an organizational belief that, as one person, one team or one project, the small things we contribute make a difference. (See Figure 18)

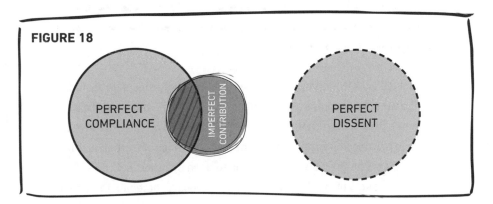

**FIGURE 18**

PERFECT COMPLIANCE

IMPERFECT CONTRIBUTION

PERFECT DISSENT

- What practices are currently in place for creating compliance? How do they work, what do they require from you and what are their effects?
- What is your sense of how these practices have been handed down to you from previous generations?
- What is the tension you, your team and your business experiences between compliance and contribution?
- Where are the people, businesses and industries that model contribution over compliance?

- What could you learn from them?
- What are the practices you could invent for creating contribution? How do they work?
- What do they require from you and what are their effects?
- When you visualize handing down new cultural practices to the next generation, what do you see? What do you hear yourself saying?

## EXPERIMENTS ARE NOT PILOTS

It is a large, complex organization that grew from its roots as an engineering business. This has left a significant imprint on the organization's language and culture and it is exhausting to do anything different without it taking a lot of energy, immense skill and a significant amount of time.

The project lead is a thoughtful and considered man, who has successfully delivered a number of complicated projects to budget and deadline. This has earned him a series of promotions to where he now sits on the executive team. The office is pristine in its appearance; there is a number of framed pictures of old project teams on the walls - they are lined up in symmetrical rows. The desk is another repository of symmetry: computer, keyboard, notepad, telephone, square blocks sitting next to each other. He gestures to the chairs in the corner of the office.

We are meeting as he has responsibility for a major part of the strategic initiative we are supporting and there is a tension between the momentum behind the project and his cultural preferences, borne out of his history within the organization. I am tired and impatient, not at my best. He slowly pours us some glasses of water and leans backwards in his chair.

"So how do you know if something of this nature is going to work or not?" I ask.

He makes a steepled hand gesture and sits back in his chair. "Well we rely on data, good, robust, quality data."

"What is the time lag between collecting the data and acting on it?"

Furrowed brow. "Conservatively, between 6-12 weeks. Well, we have to first agree on our goals, the target data, the methods we are going to use. And then have some process of data collection, often done by external partners so we have to brief them too. Then we'll sort and analyze the results before presenting them to the key decision-makers in the business with a recommendation; in a structured, systematic and scientific manner."

"And what if you needed to move more quickly?"

Pursed lips. "We wouldn't want to make any errors through haste."

My energy now lies somewhere around my ankles, I notice I am slumped in my chair and force myself to sit more upright, leaning forward. "But if you had to. Is it ever possible to act first and collect the data afterwards?"

"We wouldn't ... well, maybe we would pilot something first in a small way."

This first conversation gave us access to a whole load more pain within the project but taught us a lot. It gave us a new distinction between a pilot and an experiment that has relevance for our new organizational Age of Connection. There is much talk of experimentation in the new age of organizations without distinguishing it from what has been done for many decades in the Industrial Age – a pilot. (See Figure 19)

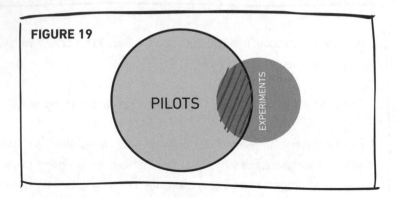

**FIGURE 19**

PILOTS

EXPERIMENTS

## HOW TO CONDUCT A PILOT

Take little risk, do something in a small way that you have already decided to do in a big way. Just learn how to do it with fewer screw-ups than you would have had if you hadn't done the pilot. Make sure you still look good during and after the pilot project reports back.

Manage your stakeholders so they are happy with the pilot result. Make a big deal of what you have learned. Above all, keep the anxiety inside you and in the system low, that is what pilots are designed to do. They are about scaling up in as efficient a way as possible from something small to something big. Pilots often come from, and then have to be fitted into, existing structures and ways of working. Being about efficiency, they often draw a boundary around the work that constrains the novel.

Many pilots already have a financial target associated with the larger-scale execution before beginning the test. That is constraining in itself. So beware - pilots end up having a lot invested in assumptions set prior to the outcomes. They are often established to confirm pre-existing biases. The data so generated can then be used to win an argument about which you were certain all along.

## HOW TO CONDUCT AN EXPERIMENT

Make lots of small bets; you don't know which, if any, will come off, the point is to learn and this may involve you looking bad, stupid or mad. If so, you should be feeling anxious and causing anxiety in the people around you. Expect messiness and lack of order; know how you will respond when this occurs and the parts of you that are likely to sabotage the experiment in the interests of neat results.

Pay little attention to your stakeholders; most of them will be encouraging you back to the norms they have put in place, defeating the point of doing an experiment. If your experiment causes stakeholders to look a little red-faced, this is a good result, know how you will manage this. This is about scaling-up from something small to something big but the scaling is focused on increasing levels of learning, not efficiency. The boundaries here don't have to be in line with what has gone before, how many unusual people and inputs could you involve in the experiment? Is there anyone you have not involved before whose opinion has been undervalued? Could this experiment just as easily produce an answer in which you will be disappointed, not the one you wanted or expected? Are there any ways in which you are using the experiment to manipulate your position? If so, you are probably doing a pilot.

Experiments strengthen the channel and help us make the transition to the Age of Connection. I don't have anything against pilots, they serve a useful purpose, I'm just arguing that the two concepts are not interchangeable. Pretending a pilot is an experiment for the fear of really experimenting.... keeps us stuck.

## FAR FROM HOME

It is the early morning rush at reception, four receptionists behind the desk, three of whom are usually harried, abrupt and keep their eyes down when checking you in. I have been coming through these doors for years saying "hello" and giving my name, there is no flicker of recognition. So I pray for my friend, the fourth receptionist, who smiles, acknowledges we have met before and always has a moment for some human contact.

It is even busier and noisier than usual.

"What's going on?" I ask, not expecting the answer I get.

"It's the Formula One car in the foyer, people can't get enough of it."

I'm curious and a little bemused, the last thing this mechanical organization needs is another machine.

I offer a few lazy, prejudiced opinions on it as my client picks me up from reception and we walk past this beautiful, logo-covered vehicle with more than a hundred pairs of eyes peering at it; people chatting animatedly to one another before starting their day's work.

"You are a creative business, wouldn't something closer-to-home be more relevant?"

The leader with whom I'm working is gushing with enthusiasm.
"I know what you mean, I was very sceptical at first, thought it must have been some kind of late-night dodgy deal drummed up in a cigar-filled room. But the business is captivated, the story is that our processes have been in need of improvement for a long time and we haven't moved fast enough. The

Formula One deal also involves a partnership where their engineers share their learning on process improvement, they are operating at a completely different level of precision to us."

The work is successful and is one example of the many times I have now experienced this phenomenon. The best sense I can make of it is that it encourages innovation and invention rather than improvement. Many businesses are in desperate need of people who can help recreate their organizations, yet, under pressure, they understandably revert to the status quo, doing their best, finding ways to improve the domain they are already in. In the Age of Connection, the successful are finding ways to access other domains, far away from their own.

When they do this, there is a spillover from one domain to the other and learning tips back the other way as well. In this case, an engineering business was learning from a creative business and vice versa.

Our fear often stops us setting foot outside our own territory, crossing the borders to explore distant lands. The blocks are self-imposed but the fears well-founded. It takes time to find and build those new relationships that lead to creative serendipity. You're not going to find them in the conferences you usually attend, the consultancies you employ or the benchmarking studies you buy. All this takes the time you don't allow yourself for fear of wasting it in fruitless exploration. The fear is also well-founded because transpositions from different worlds into your own are more likely to fail. And yet, far from home is where the Flawed but Willing usually find the relationships, insight and experience that generate invention rather than incremental improvement. (See Figure 20)

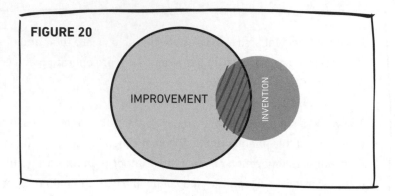

**FIGURE 20**

IMPROVEMENT

INVENTION

- How far from home can you travel? To suppliers, partners and other organizations in your own industry? To new industry sectors connected to your own or sectors that have nothing to do with your activity, business model or customer base?
- What are the interesting ways of working that you observe in these other places? Don't worry about immediate relevance, just play with the areas that grab your interest.
- How can you create connections to these distant lands? Can you create the kind of connection that may come back and re-create you?
- If you were changed by the connection and you changed them, what might you end up looking like?

## ROOM FOR THE ABSURD

They are sitting looking blankly at the flip-chart. We continue to write down the sentences as they come up, trying to quiet the chatter in our brains. This is going terribly wrong, they hate it, they hate us, have we missed the point completely. "Quick," I think, "we need to do something clever to recover this; no, breathe and stay with it, we'll be ok."

My co-facilitator is tapping his belt-buckle in the way he does when he is nervous and is swallowing a little too often to suggest he is any calmer on the inside than I am. We are playing with the distinction of being absurd using the mechanism of random questions.

Where after the others act controlling cat?
When HR cycle the strategy that reflects customers?
Why don't you hijack fruit bowls?
Why not run of car play?
Does the business avoid grey cats?
Could you deliver noisy buildings

We need to get a sentence from everyone in the room but we're not half way through yet and my stomach is screaming "stop!" But my heart is telling me it will be ok so we keep going, more buckle tapping and swallowing until we have a few more.

How would you demurely shout?
What are the unintended consequences among fluffy head office?
Why behind bright his wheelbarrow desire among loud door?
Why wall exercise furry I sad?
What lean boring goat enjoys fast house?
When they paint warm table happily I run.

Now we are sitting quietly, watching the other people in the room take in all the questions. I am reminded of Alice in Wonderland; which character used to talk in nonsense riddles? Or was it all of them? Can't remember.

How do these absurd questions give you access to the edges of your organization?

How do they help you see past the rational edge of what you currently do and tip you into the land of nonsense and impossibility?

Then something fascinating starts to happen: worrying less about their senior executive image and expertise, one person makes a connection between a sentence and their struggle on a particular project. Within minutes the room is full of verbal pictures, metaphors, rhyming couplets, laughter, identification and a host of new nicknames for some of their absent colleagues. The things that needed to be talked about are getting some airtime and because they have been approached from a fuzzy side view (not face-on, but from a hazy, irrational place, somewhere at the edge of our vision) there is a new tone to the conversation.

And then our time is up; the team members pack up their smart briefcases and file out of the room. As the last person leaves, he sticks out his suited trouser-leg in an impersonation of a 'John Cleese-style' silly walk.

Our fear of looking ridiculous and not having immediate answers often stops us challenging the status quo. The absurd questions we used are a nice vehicle, but any device will do that makes it harder to quickly pinpoint or jump to an answer. Anything that breaks the pattern of reliance on superior knowledge; that stops the brain for just long enough and asks you to sense, feel and nudge your way into a response. This all strengthens our channel as we transition to the next place. (See Figure 21)

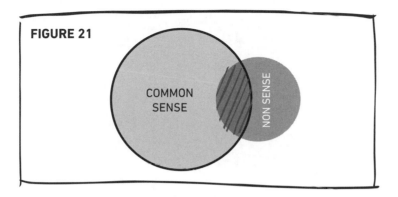

**FIGURE 21**

COMMON SENSE

NON SENSE

- What is your description of your organization's 'common sense'?
- What is the wrong thing? What is the forbidden thing?
- What are your devices for tipping yourself over into the absurd if you need to?
- What will you risk to spend some time in these places that may be seen as 'non sense'?
- How empty or meaningless do you fear it to be?
- How will you face the discomfort on the other side?

We make sense of things too quickly in the Establishment. If we build the channel strongly enough, it will hold our absurdities for a little longer than we find comfortable and then, out of the absurd, comes the elegant and novel, the path to the next phase.

# SEVEN

## Awareness

- - - - - - - - - - - - - - - - -

I wonder if the fact I am now criticizing
much less is because I have stopped looking
for the connectivity and am simply enjoying
your observations. I fell out with aspects
of this book months ago and so now I go from
one story to the next. In fact now I am doing
this I am enjoying it much more, and learning
from your stories, observations and insights.
I realise this isn't quite what you intended!

Amid the great stories again is the phrase
"strong back, soft front". I just love this. It
captures everything about managing and coping
with our lives within complex, increasingly
interconnected and uncertain business
environments. I am still playing with this idea in
my mind, dwelling on it, coming back to it.

- - - - - - - - - - - - - - - - -

# SEVEN (A)
## Practices for inside yourself

### CHURNING OUT CHARTS

He is not much older than me, dressed in the standard-issue dark blue suit, white shirt, blue tie that the consultants prefer and is welcoming me as a secondee from the client organization to his project team.

"We will work you like you have never been worked - but you will leave with an accelerated view of how to provide strategic analysis and leadership".

I was in awe of him and the rest of the team. Young, bright graduates from the places from which you are meant to graduate, machine-like in their work ethic and with access to all areas of the organization. One word from them and your career was dust, or at least that was what the gossip around the coffee machine was telling me. I watched, worked and learned, staring with disbelief as my new friends churned out charts in real-time as they were listening to a market research debrief, a team meeting conversation, reading last year's reports or often all three in the same moment. Listen, analyze, draw, and then send to the super PA back at the office who knew how to turn these scribbles into dense packs from the standard template.

These packs often became the source material that launched a thousand meetings, leaders using the insights of others as their own to demonstrate their strategic ability or justify a personal position. You just had to remember to change the slide template and cover. The problem for those who used this approach and worshipped the analysis is that they didn't then have the awareness to move position when necessary. Their awareness quotient was underdeveloped so when the inevitable happened and the original analysis was out of date, in came the consultants again to do the next round of their work.

There is undoubtedly much value to this kind of analysis and yet it is becoming more and more difficult to rely on it to transform the strategic landscape of our organizations.

I find it paradoxical that, just as it is being proved to be less effective, it is being relied upon more.

This feels particularly relevant as we picture ourselves building our channel at the edges of the Establishment, preparing ourselves for a future we cannot predict. In the absence of accurate forecasting, maybe what we have left is the development of an extreme, acute awareness; one that may allow us to pick up signals quickly and respond effectively. The limiting factors stop being a lack of vision, ideas or strategy and become ones of seeing, feeling, sensing, hearing the present moment individually and collectively.

In the Industrial Age we benefitted from our genius as human beings in understanding the science of mechanics and designing the engines that powered our economic growth. In the Age of Connection our genius may be in the fact that we are the most sensitive of all instruments, able to perceive far beyond a machine by joining with and entering into the phenomena ahead of us. A regeneration of our organizations coming through noticing and acting on the subtle changes in front of us. (See Figure 22)

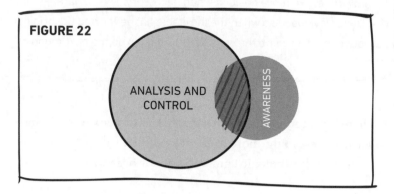

**FIGURE 22**

ANALYSIS AND CONTROL

AWARENESS

Overnight I realised that, as a leader in this organization:

I marginalize my imagination.

I look at detail, rather than seeing the process or overview.

I sanitize my relationships rather than naming any doubts or resistances or distresses.

I take all the responsibility for what is happening, rather than seeing myself as part of the whole.

So what is happening to me might be happening for you.

**(An insight left anonymously on a flip-chart after one of the Relume workshops.)**

## STRONG BACK, SOFT FRONT

His hands are the first things I notice, they seem to be lightly-clenched, even though we are talking about something relatively mild in terms of emotions. I don't recall seeing them open other than to shake hands. His body always looks as if it is leaning forward at a 20° angle and when he sits, the posture is hunched, shoulders curving forward and elevated so they stretch towards his ears. When he walks, the stride is shortened and the right foot seems to drag a little, it is placed in front of the left foot quite close into the body. The arms don't swing very much, the slightest of movements back and forth.

His breath is shallow, as if it never quite gets past the top of his chest, never touches his abdomen or flows down into the pelvic area. His forehead has three leaning lines that have been carved into it by a frown that is there about 80% of the time. This is a common sight to me, of leaders in the Establishment who have come to over rely on their cognition and who are somehow scared of feeling. Their bodies and postures are tightened around the need for constant analysis and processing of data. They have lost contact with the rest of their bodies as sources of information. They prefer not to feel or at least to claim that their feelings have no part to play in their day-to-day business choice.

When you notice this rigidity and work on changing your posture, when you stand straight, you are proclaiming to the world that it all counts. One of my colleagues calls this "having a strong back and a soft front". I love that expression for how it captures the capacity to use our bodies as a sensing mechanism. In this next phase, with the transition as uncertain as it is, we will have to rely far more on our ability to sense what is immediately in front of us than analyze what has just happened.

There is a big difference in our bodies between being rigidly alert and being gently aware. (See Figure 23)

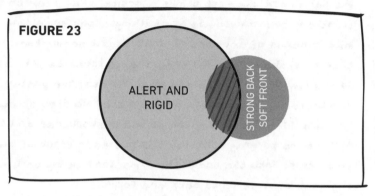

**FIGURE 23**

ALERT AND RIGID

STRONG BACK SOFT FRONT

- As you stand and look at yourself in a mirror, notice your posture and then close your eyes.
- Make some small changes, planting your feet comfortably shoulder-width apart. Allow your knees to be soft, not rigidly locked.
- As you raise your head a little, allow your chest and pelvis to rise.
- Imagine you have two eyes in the front of your neck and they need to be able to see ahead of you.
- Bring your head to a comfortable position and relax your shoulders, let them fall.
- Often, at this stage, your face is smiling; if it isn't, try out a smile and breathe gently into your body.
- Now, with a 'strong back and soft front', how is your awareness?

## SYMPTOMS AS HEALTH

My back has gone! I register that familiar feeling as I reach to tie my shoelaces and realise how little movement there is. I know what is coming in the days ahead, pain, treatment, disability, weakness, frustration, anger, and avoidance. But none of that stops me falling into an old pattern, which is to strap myself up as tight as I can and get out of the door, desperate not to disappoint the people I am meant to be meeting. On the way, I hastily arrange an appointment with the chiropractor who can't see me for a couple of days.

This time, as I lie here unable to sleep, I connect with this injury in a different way. I have woken up in the middle of the night again, each time I turn the pain jabs me and wakes me. A warm and slightly soggy blue ice pack accompanies me as I try to turn onto my side and push myself out of bed. By this point, my legs won't take any weight without me screaming so I crawl to the bathroom and heave myself up using the toilet as a crutch. And then repeat the procedure in reverse. I am glad my wife is sleeping in the other room and my children don't see me like this.

I realize what lengths I go to to keep this part of me hidden, preferring all kinds of excuses and explanations to letting those around me know what a state I am in. "Yes, of course I will get to the party at the weekend, no the drive will be fine, yes just a lot of fuss about nothing, I'll be right as rain in a couple of days." It feels overwhelming to have to accept all of its disabling and limiting factors.

It is as if it must have no airtime or voice, this disability, as if it has nothing to offer but pain and inconvenience. It stops me doing what I want, makes me look weak in the eyes of those to whom I want to look strong. It suggests I am doing something wrong myself to cause the illness and I feel a hypocrite when talking to clients about looking after their own resilience. It is those things and maybe more also - is there something in my body that is trying to express itself through my injury? What is it?

The metaphor of illness extends well to organizational health. Maybe our organizational symptoms could also be a powerful source of insight if we allowed awareness of them rather than suppression. They are commonly avoided, projected elsewhere, made a repository of blame and accusation; there is no space for the symptoms to speak about their state and point towards something new trying to emerge.

Ultimately, illness doesn't ask for permission, it manifests, it doesn't know how to introduce itself and ends up forcing itself upon us, sharply, both in our bodies and in our organizations. So maybe our work is to seek out the symptoms, amplify rather than dampen them, to help our system work with them so that they don't feel too much to cope with. (See figure 24)

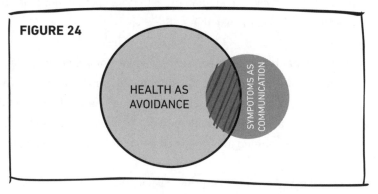

**FIGURE 24**

HEALTH AS AVOIDANCE

SYMPTOMS AS COMMUNICATION

Then what might happen?
- Where are all those places in your organizational life we are rushing past?
- Where downtime, illness, low energy, weakness and death have a place of value?
- How can you develop your awareness of what they are communicating to you?

## THE LOST PIECES

He was bringing me a whole new level of experience in the concept of denial. Our work had begun because there was persistent background noise around this senior leader's tendency to push, dominate and bully his way into making things happen. Our early experiences together showed me a fundamentally kind and caring man who had little patience with the complexities and subtleties of the large bureaucratic business his organization had become. When he joined the bank, it had been a small regional affair, but 20 years on, it had exploded into a complex global organization and his personal stock had risen with it.

He sat bolt upright in his chair, his seat higher than mine, a tall imposing figure only made more so by the clothes he was wearing.

His hair was slicked back with a fine dark shine that I imagined belied his age. His face creased with years of worry (about everything!). His desk was immaculate with the obligatory pictures of family, a little obscured by a number of other artefacts of office life. I was used to more formal (usually pinstriped) standard of dress in the banking sector but hadn't come across anyone wearing a waistcoat for many years. I felt desperately under-dressed but tried not to panic about it as I held my china teacup and we talked some more.

We had discussed a range of items in our previous sessions, his response to anything that bordered on the emotional was usually summarized with a dismissive "this is so trivial it isn't worth bothering about."

As the pressure on him to perform increased, so did the numbers of complaints about his behaviour and finally someone had issued a formal notice, which he was holding in front of him as we spoke. I imagined his voice a little more gravel-filled and slower than usual.

"I can't believe what is written here. What is she claiming?"

"Constant fault-finding, no recognition of her value to the team, that I undermine and isolate her; that the workload is overwhelming and anything good is never recognized or given credit more widely; that she carries a lot of responsibility but I won't give her the authority to go with it. She says constantly changing my mind means the finishing line is never quite the finishing line. I could go on." His voice drifts off.

"Will it go to a tribunal? HR is saying she has made a bullying claim against me."
"Are you a bully?"
"No I detest bullies, I do everything I can to stop them."
"What if you were? Is there even a small part of you that identifies with one?"
"It would have been hard not to, considering how my father brought me up."

We had talked about some of his developmental experiences in previous conversations but they were usually presented as something that had made a man of him.

"Ok - so as much as you dislike the bullying part of your father - there is a part of you that has become it?"
"Not sure."
"Let's play with it for a moment, if there was a part of you that was him in full, what would it sound like, look like? What impact would he be having?

Long silence. "Pretty much like the description in the complaint."

He apologized to his colleague and the apology had a different quality because he was able to communicate exactly how it felt to be on the receiving end of his behaviour.

Lack of awareness underlies our own fragmentation and that of our organizations. The Industrial Age has preferred a short-cut that allows us to quickly label individuals, teams and businesses as either one thing or another. It allows for initial speed and easy identification, but not always a helpful or accurate one.

In the Age of Connection we are going to have to work on integration rather than separation. It sounds obvious doesn't it?

But there is a deeper level of psychological work to be done here in order to feel both parts of yourself, the alternative polarities and be able to feel them, articulate them so that they slowly come together in a healthy way.

In the container that we are building to support our transition from one age to the next, you are stronger if you can hold both polarities rather than owning one or the other. And once you can do that you can adapt much faster in the great restructuring of our organizations. (See Figure 25)

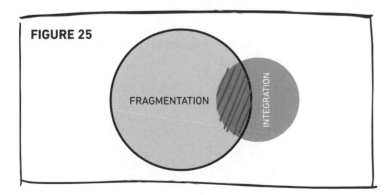

**FIGURE 25**

FRAGMENTATION

INTEGRATION

On this occasion I was working in a situation that brought together the bully and the victim in the same person. It might be alternative polarities, other examples to play with might be:

| | |
|---:|:---|
| Intelligent | Stupid |
| Sad | Happy |
| Whole | Fragmented |
| Healthy | Damaged |
| Sane | Crazy |
| Rigid | Fluid |
| Conformist | Rebel |
| Frightened | Fearless |
| Agitated | Calm |

Can you think of any others?

Try a few out for size; see how both parts feel and where they sit.

Speak them out, write them down and identify which you own and which you deny.

# SEVEN (B)
## Practices for 'between us'

### SUBTLE SIGNS

"Just observe the other," he says. "Sit opposite each other and, just for three minutes, observe everything you can. Start each observation with 'in this 'now moment' I notice'...".

I hate this stuff, it always makes me squirm, I can't even force myself to make eye contact. And it shouldn't be difficult as she is lovely. A big warm face and one of those smiley smiles that suggests she is used to doing it. My body language, on the other hand, suggests "go away" as it usually does. Ok, we are sitting opposite one another; I didn't speak up fast enough so I have to go first. I turn my chair a little more so that I am less side-on, unfold my arms, feeling cold as I do so, put my hands on my knees, lean forward slightly and begin. Where to begin? At the beginning I suppose.

"Ok... in this 'now moment' I notice...dark brown hair, shiny, long-to- your-shoulders... a round face", (can I say that or will she be offended?)..."brown eyes and a slight upturn of the mouth." The smile gets wider, I relax a little more; I keep going, describing the surface detail and then run out of things to say but I have to keep going, those are the rules...now a few moments of discomfort.... and then there is a kind of break-through as I notice another level of detail that hadn't been available to me initially.

"So, in this 'now moment' I notice.... that you are gripping the clipboard to your lap very tightly.........that you are perfectly colour-co-ordinated...the burgundy top matches the burgundy skirt and your auburn hair...there are no creases or wrinkles anywhere...your black leather bag matches your black leather boots." And then there is something else as I look more closely and with more attention at her feet.

"The boots, they are a bit of a misfit...in this 'now moment', I notice that the right shoe has a big scuff mark as if you have kicked something hard...I notice you don't appear to be someone who would kick anything.... and the boots themselves are long, with silver buckles all the way up them and the straps don't sit straight like everything else. They are curled to the side as if you have pulled them hard many times. It is as if this part of you is not as proper as everything else."

The exercise thankfully came to an end not long afterwards and the debrief was very interesting. This executive told me her story of being desperate for a less corporate and more creative career; that she was just getting in touch with this need and starting to act on it.

It struck me that, as a new phase comes to life, there are subtle signals of its emergence. The complexity scientists call them 'weak signals'. I prefer the term 'subtle' as it focuses the mind a little more on the kind of thing we are looking for. It encourages us to tune into our ways of tracking, noticing and appreciating the less obvious. I imagine that, as organizations sit at the edge between one dominant system and the new one that is trying to emerge, our capacity to notice the subtle is a key part of building the channel that will strengthen us.

So often, the subtle signals show up in our relationships and interactions with each other and our work environments. What if you were to think about them for the next day? Where do they show up? Look for something you haven't seen or noticed before but that has been present. What might it tell you about what is trying to emerge in your organization? (See Figure 26)

Could you pay more attention to:

- A tone?
- A gesture?
- A new word being used?
- A glance?
- A feeling or sensation?
- A colour?
- A reflection of the light?
- Anything that you weren't expecting, no matter how small or insignificant it may seem at the time?

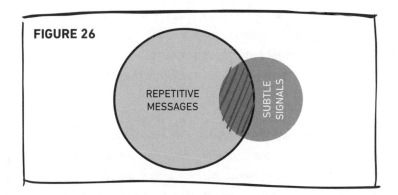

**FIGURE 26**

REPETITIVE MESSAGES

SUBTLE SIGNALS

## MICRO-RELATING

I have struggled over the years to distinguish between micro-managing and micro-relating. The people who held the CEO position before me were stone- faced, impassive, sitting at the end of the table while I presented the material; they generally monitored the numbers and then they would be the people who finally passed judgements. Their judgements were sometimes half-heartedly challenged but mostly there was little argument.

I learned some things from them but what struck me most, and scared me most, in taking their chair was how dull they were. They could manage a business at a minute level of detail but few of them went on to do anything interesting with their lives when they left here. And they left with very little understanding of how this organization really worked. Why would they? They hadn't ever tried to understand the guts of it.

Their power stemmed from the collective power of the company, I would like my situation to be the other way around; I want to contribute to the collective power of the company. It may be a prejudice but many of these old CEOs came from a finance background, their experience was helpful in times of mergers and acquisitions. They were able to understand the complexity and technical jargon of the numbers to the satisfaction of the city but were missing other needed qualities.

So I chose something different as an approach. I didn't want to micro-manage but I did want to micro-relate and micro-engage. I don't mean the kind of engagement that comes from someone else managing your internal and external profile, I mean the kind that comes with trying to shift things in your organization by throwing yourself into the system. I don't believe you can understand any business properly until you have tried, personally, to change some aspect of it. At that point, you have become part of the complexity for real, you are no longer sitting at the end of the table. All that emerges, all that you didn't intend, all that leaves you powerless, all the struggles and learning from opinions that are different to your own.

There are many judgements passed about this kind of leadership that suggest this is not your CEO role, that you are 'micro-managing' but it has a different quality. The best I can come up with is this phrase 'micro-relating'. I am not telling people in detail what to do; I am trying to experience, in detail, what it is like. It will never be perfect, because of the power that comes with my role, but it is a start, and as people get used to working with me in this way, they defer less and give me the real version of events more often. (See Figure 27)

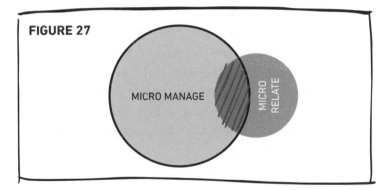

**FIGURE 27**

MICRO MANAGE

MICRO RELATE

- What habits do you have that enable you to deaden or reduce the full level of engagement? How do you defend against this?
- What does experiencing life directly mean to you in the context of your business?
- What might you choose from your current priorities that could give you this quality of experience?
- How would you arrange things with your colleagues so that it didn't default to 'pleasing the boss'?

- What are some of the ways, in which you could develop this personal capacity to micro-relate?

## COMMUNITIES OF PASSION

As a senior leader in the organization, she is perfectly capable; in the Industrial Age you wouldn't want to lose her. Committed to her work, she strives to improve her standards; customers and colleagues love what she delivers. There is no excessive praise from them but she doesn't drop a big problem in your lap either. Learning happens through a range of mechanisms but it is mostly because someone has asked her to go on a course or read something or attend a particular meeting. She is keen to share and learn about best practice and bring it into her work. All of it is done with a smile and the few complaints she has about the organization are to do with being overloaded, not having enough time at home, taking too much responsibility for the other, less capable people around her. The communities set up around her are communities of practice, setting up and improving the way things are today.

She has decided, after many months of agonizing, that there is no point carrying on with this role and this organization. It was a hard choice to make but it sounded as if, emotionally at least, she was now ready and determined. Her face was pinched in at the sides and her thin, wiry build oozed lean, efficient strength. She needed it, like many women of her generation she was a successful senior executive, mother and wife who had as much demand on her at home as she did at work. It took a supreme time-management effort to cope and there wasn't a spare moment in the day. She often sacrificed her own wellbeing and the coaching sessions with me were a regular casualty of her 'time management'.

"This hurts like I have fallen out of love with a partner. It happened a while ago, but I have been trying to convince myself it was just a blip, that it would be ok eventually. It isn't getting better, it is getting worse."

So our attention turns to the future and finding a job and an organization with which she can fall in love again.

"Do you know any good headhunters?"
"Yes but to be honest they are less useful than exploring your own network".
"I don't have one of those".
"Huh?"
"I don't have a network outside this place, I've been working in the same organization for almost twenty years!"
"What about all those people who worked here that have now left?"
"I get lots of invites from some of them on this LinkedIn thing."
"Great! So you do have a network then."
"Well, no, I tend to say no to the requests. I'm always worried people want something from me or are trying to sell me something I don't want or will get me to spend time on things that I don't have".
"Hmm. Which was the most recent of these?"
"An old team member of mine had left to set up their own marketing consultancy and they invited me to a conference on the impact of social media on brand marketing."

"I would like to suggest an experiment."
"Ok."
"For the next four weeks I would like you to say yes to every request that comes your way, any invitation, any connection and any opportunity. It is quite possible that you are right – 50% of these may be a waste of time when considered from your old mindset. Our new mindset is saying "yes" to the connections. Everyone you meet is part of your network and you make the first

move to contact them after the meeting."

"Sounds uncomfortable. I'll give it a go if I have the time."

I arch an eyebrow quizzically in my best impression of Sean Connery but know it is probably closer to Rowan Atkinson as both my eyebrows will be raised while I scrunch up the right side of my face.

"Err ok- I get it. I will give it a go."
"Great, thank you."

"One more thing – please return to everyone you said no to on LinkedIn, apologise and ask them to connect with you."

A few months later, there is a new version of the same woman sitting in front of me and, interestingly, she has chosen not to leave her organization. She is passionately ready for the next stage of her career and has accessed this through a new level of interpersonal awareness. Now the organization doesn't feed her as much as she feeds the organization through her connection to her interests.

She always has a side interest on the go; it is connected to her work but not necessarily driven by it. It is a place where she poses a question, a stimulating thought, something that is sparking her interest and curiosity at the moment. And then she relies on her sources of connection to the world inside and outside her organization. Through social media and personal relationships she can bypass many of the institutional barriers that our Industrial Age leader had as blocks.

She can take a question, stimulate ideas from her virtual network, use the same connections to bring together some resources and try something out.

It isn't hard work; when you watch her in action, it feels more like play with a purpose. She has become a one person research and development lab, taking something from discovery to testing to development, often without it touching the formal organizational structures; quickly she has something that impacts her day-to-day work and can then be brought back into the business. (See Figure 28)

**FIGURE 28**

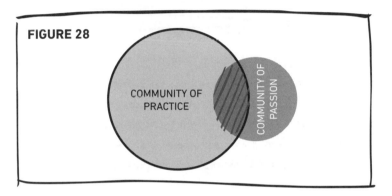

- How are you exploring your passions and interests outside of work?
- How are you rewarding yourself and those around you for developing connections outside of the organization?
- How can you support individual initiative in this area even when you don't see an immediate or direct connection to their work objectives?
- What are the inquiries and experiments that are part of your 'research plan'?

# SEVEN (C)

## Practices for across us all

LYING UP THE HIERARCHY [6]

I spent 10 years of my life writing. I wrote plans, partnership strategies, the Local Area Agreement, stretch targets, the Sustainable Community Strategy, sub-regional infrastructure plans, funding bids, monitoring documents and service plans. These documents described the performance of our business and its partners.

I have a confession to make. Much of it was made up. It was fudged, spun, copied and pasted, cobbled together and attractively-formatted. I told lies in themes, lies in groups, lies in pairs, strategic lies, operational lies, cross-cutting lies. I wrote hundreds of pages of nonsense. Some of it was my own, but most of it was collated from my colleagues across the organization and brought together into a single document; this was my specialty and my profession.

Why did I do it? I did it because it was my job. My manager told me it was to "to get the best for the region" and that "you have to play the game". When I attempted to reveal the absurdity of the situation I was criticized for not being in the real world. I quickly learned that, in the real world, data is cleansed, re-presented and re-formatted until it tells an acceptable and neat story.

My can-do attitude was rewarded with promotion in the hierarchy and respect from my colleagues. Stretching the truth was seen as harmless and normal. Our behaviour was rational. We told lies in order to:

- Win funding
- Keep management teams happy
- Impress European departments
- Gain a good rating annually
- Compete with other organizations in our region

The purpose of our behaviour was to maximize the chances of looking good and to minimize the chance of upsetting or embarrassing important people in the hierarchy.

Am I exaggerating? My use of the word 'lying' is intentionally provocative, but if not lying, we certainly weren't confident that what we were writing represented reality. We made huge assumptions about the link between the data we collected and the experience of the user. We made similarly outrageous assumptions about the impact of our interventions on performance.

There was always a kernel of truth in what we wrote and the intentions were good. However, the purpose of the written work was to project coherent, positive news. Projects were rarely abandoned, mistakes rarely made and uncertainty never expressed. Nothing ever happened by chance, no issue was complex, little understood or messy. Our projects were almost always on track and we apparently had complete control of the future. We even knew the outcome of our work before we started it. Everything was robust, nothing flimsy. We told stories, rationalized the past, projected an ambitious image and made anything bad look good or under control. The truth even had to be re-told to fit two sides of A4, the standard quarterly reporting template. Later, when we had performance management software, the lies were shorter – no more than 50 words; the space allocated in the progress box on the screen.

When anomalies were discovered in our data, it was treated as a technical problem or a problem of co-ordination. Serious attempts were made by talented and well-paid people to improve data quality and to embed a robust performance management framework. These attempts did nothing to change the underlying thinking. The purpose of collecting and reporting data was to comply, not to learn. Compliance was systemic and learning was optional and ad hoc.

We were preoccupied with meeting targets, demonstrating the achievement of outcomes and avoiding embarrassment.

I was not a liar outside work and neither were my colleagues.Even lying itself was cleansed and reclassified into the phrase 'playing the game'. Context can fool us into doing extraordinary things.

The alternative to lying to the hierarchy is simple. Take the hierarchy to see the truth.

We should have taken our leaders to see what was actually going on. We should have persuaded them to sit for days at a time, to listen to hours of phone calls from the public and to understand service users in their own contexts. Only then would they begin to understand the true performance of the organization. Performance officers do not need to spend whole days tinkering with text and formatting reports, mediating reality into something palatable. There is no need for an expensive bureaucracy between the decision-makers and the truth. Confronting the brutal facts is free.

To find out what is really going on across an organization, you don't need to know which version of a report you are reading, there are no approvals necessary, no checking, nothing cross-cuts and nothing comes in clusters or themes. It is just as it is. Always there, waiting to be discovered; immediate, live and real.

There are no lies here. At the bottom of the hierarchy, where the end-user touches it, you find out the truth. This is the secret of which many in senior positions aren't able to convince themselves yet. If you want to understand the whole organization, enter the experience very deeply at a small and local level. This will give you all the awareness you need. (See figure 29)

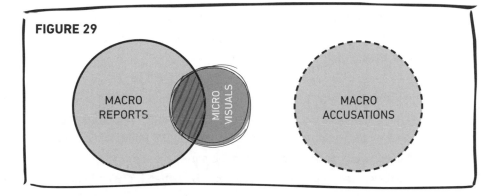

**FIGURE 29**

MACRO REPORTS

MICRO VISUALS

MACRO ACCUSATIONS

## WORKING AT THE CORE

I have spent years feeling the need to regain my fitness and lose weight. I usually start going to the gym, getting really sweaty, making a lot of noise, feeling a bit better but soon return to my starting position. Last year, things started to get worse when I had operations on my knees.

I started Pilates and, since January, I have attended twice a week. This work focuses on the core and builds strength from the inside out. The instructors focus on fine movements. They do not compromise on finding and building the core. The movements and their interventions are subtle and not at all macho but the results are extraordinary and sustainable. If you strengthen the core, you just get stronger and more stable.

I have been thinking about Pilates as a metaphor for strengthening our organizations and, in particular, strengthening mine. The idea of two different kinds of strength is captivating: one developing the core, from the inside, the other developing the surface, from the outside. I suppose we are good at the latter, we have learned how to create and present an image of ourselves through the disciplines of management that make us look strong. Yet often that strength is exposed as insufficient to meet the demands of today. In particular, I notice now that very visibly muscular people can also have a frailty around their backs and knees.

When I think about working on the core I find myself noticing the small-but-significant movements and trying to find ways of strengthening them and the people behind them. The difference between me and the Pilates instructor is that she doesn't compromise on finding the core. I often do, allowing myself to be distracted by pressures of the day. But when I reflect on our progress, I realise it has been through small, subtle, repetitive movements that strengthen us. There are strong parallels with business. We work hard on big, noisy and sweaty movements that compromise the core. They look big and important but when the focus on them stops the jelly returns to its original shape very quickly.

As I work more with the principles of Pilates, I see many other parallels. It is about reminding your body how to really work, generating a connected flow of energy throughout the body. (See figure 30)

- What are all the big movements in your organization that are designed to build a 'six-pack' that everyone can see?
- What are the small movements that are strengthening the core of your organization, which may not be visible but generate hidden stability?
- How can you develop your awareness of the small movements that are providing an unseen stability at the core of the organization?
- How can you amplify them so that they are more effective and better supported?

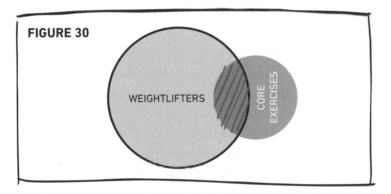

**FIGURE 30**

WEIGHTLIFTERS

CORE EXERCISES

## BE INSIDE THE FRAME

We are standing looking at a named piece of art in the National Gallery in London. With me is a coaching client, someone repeatedly looked over for promotion from director to vice president (VP). In this organization, this career shift seems to be the most difficult and most prized. It is almost as if, before it, you have achieved nothing and after it, you can relax, full of achievement. She is understandably confused that, despite having achieved stellar ratings on her annual appraisals and constant assurances of her value to the organization, no-one seems willing to back her for the next move.

The walls of the gallery are deep red, providing a fetching contrast to the heavy, gilded frames and the ageing wooden floor. We are in front of a 15th century work of art with a religious theme, not to my taste, by a Dutch artist. I challenge myself to stop being so narrow-minded and open my filters, even if just briefly. The security guard in the corner has a look of disdain and boredom directed into thin air. We are visiting in office hours, on a weekday outside of school holidays, so this extends us the luxury of being able to sit on one of the black sofas, without a back to rest on, and contemplate the painting from a distance.

My client is reflecting on the feedback recently received about why she didn't get the last VP role for which she applied. "Not strategic enough" was the feedback provided. When we explore what she understands by this, she is confused and a little hurt, her brow is furrowed. The way she has been taught about strategy seems to be what she follows faithfully: Analysis to identify the profitable markets in which to compete and clarify what winning in a market looks like; identifying or creating unique strengths compared to competitors; and leading the execution in such a way that the elements that need managing are managed.

It sounds pretty good to me and yet, as we sit in front of this work, the things that are missing become a little clearer. I have asked her to interpret this piece of art using the skills she uses when interpreting a market or new brand launch. It's all perfectly reasonable. Then we have another attempt. This time, I am asking for a personal connection of a different nature to the analytic connection that has just been completed. (See Figure 31)

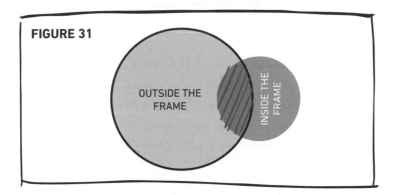

**FIGURE 31**

OUTSIDE THE FRAME

INSIDE THE FRAME

- What is your personal encounter with this work?
- What does this trigger in you?
- How is it connected to your life story?
- How is it connected to the communities you are part of?
- How many different kinds of meaning can you generate and allow to unfold?
- What are all the connections you can create between this piece of art and the rest of the gallery?
- Return to the work over and again; what are the other perspectives we can view this from?
  - outside the frame
  - inside the frame
  - as the artist
  - as the commissioning client
  - as the subject matter
  - as the characters in the piece
  - as the non-living artefacts

## CHECKING IN

The group with which we are working is in the process of 'checking in' before its two days together. I can recall when I first encountered this strange term and the novel practice that followed. It intrigued me at the time that, when done well, it changed the outcomes of the meeting that followed.

What I have just experienced feels a long way from that time. There were lots of subtle signals in the room that suggested that, as the check-in progressed, it was met by impatience rather than increased awareness of one another and the collective environment that was being created. Some of the individuals had their bodies slightly turned away from the person speaking, there were lots of tight necks, hunched shoulders and an almost imperceptible shaking of the head in response to some of what was being said; pursed lips, stone faces and short statements. This had become something mechanical and habitual for this team, something to get out of the way before the real business of the day could be dealt with; short, clipped and the bare minimum.

The emotions in the room around this simple process, (judgement, cynicism, fear and guilt), were palpable.

The population was multi-national and the accepted convention was broken when a slight man from India, someone at the edges of the project, spoke for longer than those who preceded him. The response from the group was amplified and left him embarrassed, as if he had taken up too much space. The remaining people were now in even more of a rush, there was less listening and people starting to talk over one another.

The day that followed was a difficult one and we were facing a second day with too much left to do in the time available. We took a risk and reflected back on the beginning of day one. What would it be like, we wondered, if there was a little more space and good intention around the day's check-in?

After some grumbling and anxiety about the time remaining, the group began. One-by-one we heard some of what people needed to voice; where they had come from, what had brought them here, their full names and titles, how to pronounce them well, their particular interest in the project, what they feared and their pre-existing connections with other people in the room. We were showing ourselves to each other, the conversation was less formal and even joyful at times.

The additional intimacy in the room led to a different quality of conversation on day two and we achieved more in less time. The relationship with the work changed as awareness of each other was deepened.

As our work continued with this team, we experimented with ways of deepening their check-in process, it became an organizing principle for their work.

- We could have no pre-determined agenda and determine it according to what we are sensing at the beginning of the meeting.
- We could ask people for what they felt and sensed as well as for their analysis and judgement.
- We could ask each other what we would say right now if we had no fear of being judged by our colleagues or ourselves.
- We could introduce terms that were unvoiced or un-owned by the Establishment and give them

a place in our language; terms such as joy, excitement, fear, anger and sadness.

- We could take moments of silence to check-in on our bodies and see how they are trying to tell us something.
- We could practise ways of standing straight, using a 'strong back and soft front' to help increase our awareness.
- We could allocate time in the conversation that was simply about being aware of what was going on and not trying to explain it away; to let it be. (See Figure 32)

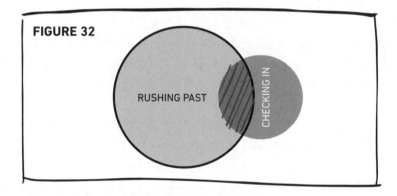

**FIGURE 32**

RUSHING PAST

CHECKING IN

The first few times I tried these experiments with this group we experienced lots distractions. Lots went on to keep us from being aware: slaps on the back, raucous laughter, teasing each other, diversion to electronic devices, sudden crises that had to be managed by leaving the room and even falling asleep!

And then, after some practice, we had access to a completely different level of conversation. We started practising this awareness before each agenda item, it changed what was talked about, how it was talked about, the speed with which choices were made and, most critically for this team, the sustained cohesion after the collective decision.

The link between collective awareness and outcomes was the closest thing to magic I have experienced.

# EIGHT

## Gentleness

---

Hard to articulate, but I suppose, don't read it like a business book and look for the structure, themes and key messages (the critical eye - which most of your reviewers seem to have done including me), but instead read it without trying to make sense of it and stuff will pop out that hits an emotion or past feeling; then stop and make sense of what it means. Some bits of the book have really hit me at an emotional level (which of course is what stories do brilliantly) other bits not at all. I imagine this is something like the reactions people get to abstract art where the meaning comes from the person and not the artist per se. Sounds a bit pretentious but the art is medium for sense-making and not the sense-making in itself... that is how this chapter and the book as a whole strikes me.

What I struggle with is what and how much conceptual stuff you are holding in the background and whether me making links to my own might be helpful or just another distraction. It may have been more helpful to lay these out more clearly?

---

# EIGHT (A)
## Practices for inside myself

### WHEN NOTHING ELSE WORKS

I am talking to a board member of a corporate multi-national as she tells me about her plans to change their impact on the environment for the better. She is well-groomed and has an easy way of talking about the superficial. I suspect this has come from many years of corporate networking where engagement is less important than exchange. She hears what I say and then responds in a way which shows me she heard but the response feels hollow somehow. She makes her excuses as she has five minutes' preparation time left before delivering her keynote presentation.

Half-way through the presentation, we have learned about her personal history and how she came to be involved in this work; to what the business is committed; how it is combining the need for profit with the need for inclusion, especially in her home country of India. I am being lulled into a drowsy state of passive acceptance when something she says wakes me up just a little.

"Our increased environmental profile is bringing many active, passionate youngsters to our business, but when I follow up with them a year or two afterwards they have succumbed to the status quo. I am left disappointed and I don't know what is happening here."

Members of the audience are shifting in their seats and there are some silent looks being exchanged that don't feel very positive to me. I wonder how this is happening. They should be fascinated and engaged in this presentation, they have invested time and money to be here, yet the energy in the room suggests they want her to stop talking and to leave. Some angry, whispered side conversations are starting to spring up in the room.

Then it hits me. She is describing a top-down vision for this change, from the top of a business that is at the top of its industry that is at the top of this movement for environmental change... but I can't feel her in it. The words are full of care for humanity and I can't feel her in them.

There is no personal experience that underpins her top-down vision. So we are left feeling disconnected. She has plenty of personal stories but little contact in those stories to the world she wants to create.

The negative reaction in the room reaches a crescendo when she says: "We don't want to give things up, I know I don't want to, not my shoes or my pension plan, and neither do any of you, so this leaves us with a complex predicament".

We don't feel her in the conversation until the very end of the questions and answers session. She is describing a long series of ways in which she maintains her resilience in the face of an organization that resists the change for which she is responsible.

"When nothing else works I remind myself that I am human."
The room breathes a collective sigh and there is a pin drop silence as we take her in and make contact again.

That could have been the starting point of her vision and presentation, not the ending.

Maybe this needs to be the starting point for all our adventures into the novel and edges of The Establishment.

It is less slick, more vulnerable in a gentle way. It is a way in which we can make connections deeply enough and quickly enough to engage the real interest of those whose support we need.

- What is the personal experience that underpins your over-arching vision for change?
- If there isn't one how will you find one?
- Where is your gentle humanity in the vision?
- How can you better frame your personal desires, limitations and struggles?

You will know it when you touch it. You will feel different on the inside and tell the story in a new way on the outside. It will focus on who you are behind the corporate persona and will include much of what you personally struggle with. (See Figure 33)

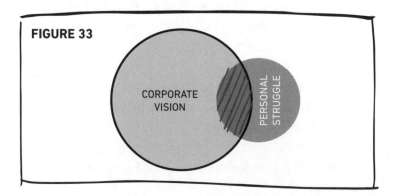

**FIGURE 33**

CORPORATE VISION

PERSONAL STRUGGLE

## ACHING HEART

The experience of being with him is like being in one very long interruption made up of many small ones. He is twitching, looking at his phone every few minutes, jumping to answer it when it rings, often just to say he is in a meeting and will call back later. He injects the conversation we are trying to have with humour that makes everyone laugh but also distracts from the issue at hand.

Always in a rush, never on time for any of our meetings, he prides himself on the extraordinary workload he is juggling. He forgets my name in an instant and finds it hard to hold eye contact for long when we do meet. A smile comes regularly to his face; reserved for all those at whom he has to smile, but doesn't really want to.

He jumps up to refill his coffee cup and comfort-eat another muffin, just a small one. The meeting finishes as it always does - early - so some time can be clawed-back for the next urgent thing that has just landed on his agenda. I notice that what I sense in him is the same thing that other people sense: irritation. And then, just behind that, pain - of a quality I can't describe. One day we have a chance to work together on the pain as it expresses itself in his body.

"My neck and shoulder have hurt for a long time. It is only on the left side - it makes me want to jerk my shoulder back so that it clicks," he says. "Or turn my neck for a similar click higher up. It is becoming a compulsion - when I do it I get some immediate relief but it tips into a series of repeating clicks until something takes my mind off it."

I ask him to stay on this subject and we explore the symptom, trying to describe in detail what it feels like. He is becoming more uncomfortable; there won't be much time before he switches his attention. I am watching him rotate his shoulder.

'When you click you grimace; you also close your eyes".
"Really?"
"Yes, it makes we wonder whether there is a part of this that is about privacy and distaste?"

He laughs.

"Now I am thinking of you on the toilet!" I say.
"Please!"
"OK but is there something private about this movement?"
"I don't know."
"Let's keep following it."

He does it again.

"Now I want to click my neck left-to-right, at the same time I keep following the sensation. It doesn't go anywhere in the same form but I notice I am standing straight with my chest out and breathing more deeply."
"You have your left hand on your side."

This is new so we bring our attention there.

"It hurts - a kind of stabbing pain. If I put my hand flat against it,the pain goes away."

"Do that again, take away your hand and put it back again."
"As I take my hand away I notice my energy dip, I feel more irritated and aggressive. When I put it back I feel peaceful."

He continues rubbing the side of his stomach and his neck feels better.

"Could you lift your hand a little? Maybe you aren't rubbing your stomach, it might be your heart."

It is unusual for corporate leaders to feel their way into thinking something new. They would rather think their way into feeling something new. They focus so much on cognition they forget about the importance of their feelings, particularly heartache. And heartache is a helpful, if painful, way of gaining insight into the struggles of the transition. If we allow it a place in the corporate conversation, the seeds of the solution may be in the problem, if only we can open ourselves fully to it, with all the heartache that will involve.

- Under gentle examination - what is your heartache?
- What is unwelcome in the heartache?
- What may be trying to emerge?
- How might it be helpful here?

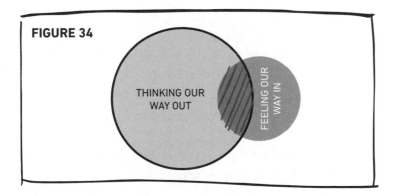

**FIGURE 34**

THINKING OUR WAY OUT

FEELING OUR WAY IN

## FAIL HAPPY

When I was 16 years of age I came under the influence of the family of a school friend. They were everything that I fantasized a family could be, in direct contrast to my belief about my own at the time. This led to me spending as much time as possible with them and I ended up 'adopted' in an informal sense. I was probably less welcome than I imagined, being there at all hours, but was happily oblivious to that.

They were a devout Christian family and this friendship eventually resulted in my being co-opted into their Sunday evening youth club run by the local vicar. I guess, looking back, I was a conversion target to their faith but, in my naive mind, I was simply enjoying the company of other teenagers, having a laugh every Sunday night.

The highlight of my time with them was being asked to take part in their annual amateur pantomime production which, that year, was to be Aladdin, I ended up with the part of the emperor. Although the vicar's daughter ended up with the plum role of Aladdin, the emperor was a relatively challenging role with plenty of lines for me to learn.

Opening night and the church was full: somehow we had managed to sell all the tickets and the press of bodies was heating up the old gothic stone church on the high street. A local company had donated lights and sound so the production had a professional feel to it and we were ready for our first performance.

There was one particular line I had to deliver, following the stage direction to "lie down on my imperial sofa at the edge of the stage".

"All citizens of China will be forced to pay extra taxes in order to pay for the best food and wine in the land."

Only, this opening night, someone had placed the sofa too close to the edge and my sitting down caused the whole thing (and me) to fall off-stage mid-sentence, disappearing into the gloom with a thump.

I lay there, slightly bruised, highly embarrassed, trying to recall my next line. I slowly lifted my head above the stage to be greeted with a wall of laughter that didn't stop for five minutes. I was a hit and a star was born. Despite my best efforts to convince him otherwise, the vicar wouldn't let me repeat the feat on future nights.

It was a strange combination of feelings. One of my colleagues talks about a desired state for teams in complex transitions and that is to 'fail happy'.[7] I imagine that acting experience was one of the few times I have understood in my body quite what that means. I had failed and I was happy, not only was I happy, the whole church was also happy as a result of my error.

I wish we all had enough gentleness towards ourselves to enable us to 'fail happy' on a regular basis. Whenever we are fearful, avoidant, blaming, self-hating or antagonistic in our failures, we could all do with summoning our own version of the internal emperor.

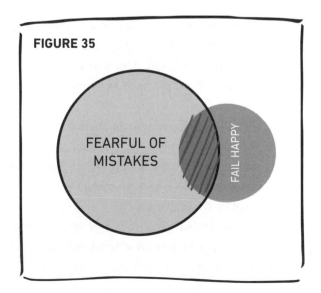

**FIGURE 35**

FEARFUL OF MISTAKES

FAIL HAPPY

## INNER THEATRE

The room is long and stark, but in a peaceful way, with a floor-to-ceiling window all the way down one side. I wonder what this conference must look like to anyone peeking in, there must be 200 of us milling around the room, exchanging a few words with one person before we move and find our next partner and repeat the same words to them.

I am taking part in the exercise, having suggested it as a way in which we could replicate an aspect of the unseen, unexpressed emotional environment in which our leaders have to operate every day. Each person has been asked to articulate the positive voice and negative voice inside their head about the particular project with which this group of 200 is tasked.

The sentences have to start with 'you', replicating what the internal voice would be saying. My voices are "you know can do anything you put your mind to" and "you don't really want to be here, this will be dull and exhausting."

When confronted with someone else's inner voice it is hard not to feel it is commenting on you. After a few exchanges, I am absorbed by the emotional waves inside me and around me and amazed how real the reactions feel, forgetting I am doing an exercise, being stung by some of what is offered.

"You are so lazy and useless what makes you think you can succeed?"
"You are interesting to others, they stop and listen to your ideas."
"You always finish what you start, it is a great quality."
'You are never afraid to try something new."
'You're not like everyone else here."
'You work with these people but they don't really like you."
'You are really good at recovering from disappointments."
'You're fine on your own, you don't need them."

'You won't be recognized for your work, you never are."
'The only reward for good work is more work."
'You are too old for this."

It is an amplified, but powerful, proxy for what it feels like to work on this project at the moment across the whole population of 200. Then we stop for a moment and take on a new practice before returning to the exercise. This time, anytime we feel moved or unbalanced by what has been said to us we stop and develop a new, gentler response. We stand in front of each other, looking at the other person, or with our eyes closed, and breathe in the difficulty from the other person.

I imagined it as a dark, heavy, hot texture and then breathed out again, imagining something lighter and cooler; something that reconnected us and promoted a sense of kindness, clarity and spaciousness. When complete, we moved to the next partner. There was no conversation about the difficulty, where it belonged or an analysis of its sources; just a gentle awareness that it was there and we could use ourselves as an echo chamber of some kind; hearing it, processing it, sending it back feeling different.

Months later, I noticed a connection between those who loved this practice and found some way of making it work day-to-day and those who contributed most, in terms of leadership, to the success of the project. It was as if they were able to see and make connections and opportunities out of whatever arose; in my story this is because they had a gentle response to the difficulties that could operate beyond what was going on in their ego.

There are furrowed brows; lots of that hyperactivity that suggests people need to be seen to be doing something. They have stumbled into a regulatory nightmare in one of the Asian countries and he has flown over to be with them. I was working with the team as this most recent difficulty unfolded and had the experience of hanging out, doing what I could to help and getting some insight from watching him operate. Imagine a room full of senior people all triggered by the stress they are under, creating dramas at every turn, worried for their own security and about the mistakes that may have been made. They feel resentful towards the corporate centre that our protagonist represents; they didn't heed the early warnings and now the company may be kicked out of the region completely.

There is an anxiety associated with what can and cannot be said in the public forum of the team and lots of side conversations that take place in the corridor; they seem to be more legitimate somehow.

I picture him in the middle of it all, people rushing past, snatched pieces of conversations that never seem to finish, claim and counter-claim, quick changes in status and power that are happening in a moment and still he keeps smiling, listening, responding.

I notice something else: he pulls himself upright, head almost elevated, opens his body to the person speaking and takes a breath - almost as if he is breathing them in and breathing them out. It sounds a bit weird but looked very natural. I ask him about that afterwards.

"I found, in these situations in the past, that I was literally holding my breath, it was like a kind of panic reaction to the stress. When I did breathe it was very shallow, the air was getting stuck in my chest but not making it down into my lungs, diaphragm, pelvic area. So I focused on it more, my breathing seems to bring a calmness to me and to the situation I am in, I believe it affects everyone in the room somehow. I have taken it a step further now, in my mind's eye I imagine that on the 'in-breath' I am taking in the stress and anxiety around me; on the 'out- breath' I am reconnecting with the person, repairing some the damage this much stress causes to the relationship." (See Figure 36)

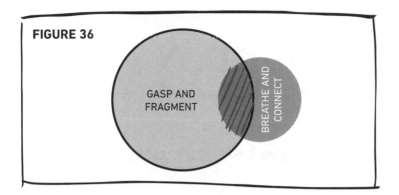

**FIGURE 36**

GASP AND FRAGMENT

BREATHE AND CONNECT

# EIGHT (B)

## Practices for between us

### GET A DOG

The conference was 10 years ago; I can't recall any of the data presented or any of the key messages they spent so long honing and delivering. I can't remember which fancy hotel we were staying in or exactly which colleagues had left the organization by then. I can't remember the food we ate.

I recall one aspect of that conference: it was the CEO and his presentation or, more specifically, one line of it. The room was dark, we were sitting in neat rows, line upon line of the audience comprising the brightest and best, the most senior leaders of the organization ready to be inspired, guided and provoked.

"You don't come to work to be loved," he said, hands on his hips standing upright behind a Perspex lectern. "If you want to be loved, get a dog."

There was much guffawing around the room, he had hit the right frequency for this audience, there was tough work to be done in the months ahead and they were all straining at the leash to show just how tough they could be. Knowing grins were exchanged and the audience leaned forward as one to hear what was next.

I recall not hearing another word that was said, I just sat there stunned in the audience. I think I almost lost faith in the organization that day. I wanted to stand up and scream "bullshit!" before flouncing out of the ballroom we were seated in. I didn't, I waited until the end and left with everyone else as the lights came up to the accompaniment of Queen's *It's A Kind of Magic*. I didn't have the guts to voice any disagreement at the party or dinner that followed, I stayed quiet and listened to all the tough talk around me.

I have experienced some profound moments in my career since the events described above and they have all been within a setting of teams that loved one other. We don't talk about it in those terms in corporate life I know, maybe words such as care and kindness are a good substitute for what I mean. This is much of the promise of the Age of Connection.

Over a short period of time we can create something between us if we talk at the right level about the things that have most meaning for us. It means all the rules, regulations and contracts that we rely on to keep us in check are hardly needed. We do not need to manufacture something called collaboration, it just arises naturally somehow. We keep pinching ourselves – how are we so cohesive without many rules and hierarchies being enforced? And after projects end we are all desperate to recreate that environment in the next team we work with.

Do the people who are working on your project care for, and take care of, each other? That turns out to be the best predictor of something novel emerging from the edges; much more so than anything that legislates for collaboration or creativity. (See Figure 37)

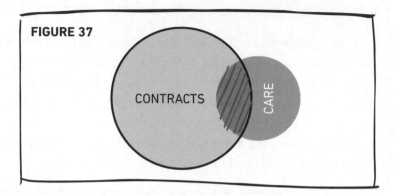

**FIGURE 37**

## LOOKING DOWN ON US

He has such good intentions, and such lack of success that my heart bleeds for him. Wanting to connect, inspire and empower the hundreds of people he is leading to great feats of invention, collaboration and courage. He knows the job won't be easy; he has recently joined an organization that has been struggling for a while. It is in that no man's land of realizing change is necessary to avoid collapse but being scared of acting for fear of the recrimination that has been present in the past.

The issue we are struggling with together today is the lack of people stepping forward with their ideas, despite his assurances that he doesn't care how stupid the suggestions may seem on the surface or how small their impact may be.

He is exhausted of saying the same thing over and over again and today we stumble on something that may be helpful.

We are experimenting with questions of status, hypothesizing that there is something about the status difference between him and others in his business that is causing a blockage to response. Of course, there is a natural status that comes with the position but we are curious about more than that. We stand looking at our reflections in the large expanse of glass that makes up one wall of the office looking out onto the security gate through which cars come in and out of the facility. The nights have drawn in; in the late afternoon, the office lights and dark evening allow us to use the window as a makeshift mirror.

I ask him to speak out loud and listen to himself at the same time; to repeat his last request for input that was made from a stage in the auditorium.

"What do you see and hear as you listen to yourself?"
"Hard to say."
"Go on have a go."

He starts describing his appearance; it is a bit too literal, we are stuck now.
"Let me have a go at playing you and you tell me what hits you."

I draw myself up a couple of inches taller and straighter and do my best to impersonate him.

This time a different quality of observation shows up.
"Your speech is quite clipped."
"You are articulate."
"You are taller than me."
"There are no 'umms' and 'ahhs' or any kind of hesitation as you speak."
"Your appearance is manicured.
"Your clothes fit well - you have taken time to co-ordinate."
"Your legs are shoulder-width apart - you look balanced and stable as you stand."
"You are willing to voice an opinion, make a demand."
"You process information very quickly and form an opinion that often sounds like it has weight of evidence behind it."

We imagined what effect those outward expressions may have on his accessibility and the ability of others to voice anything of perceived value.

We both lapse into introspection, I leave him for a while, wondering about my own interactions. As we sit quietly together, I notice one other aspect of our contact. As he looks at me his head is turned slightly to the right, with his left ear pointing towards me. He gives the impression of having to look out of the corner of his left eye. I wonder if I am imagining it but there is also a hint of his left lip turned up in a light snarl. I feel under examination in some way and we play with this idea for a while.

"Could you try changing your position as we talk so that you do the opposite? Turn your head to the left, point your right ear at me and look out of the corner of your right eye."

He tries the new position.

"It feels very uncomfortable, very unnatural, like I have to force myself into this position. It takes an effort to hold it here even though, in theory, it is such an easy physical movement."

"OK hold it for a little longer and see if anything starts to emerge in your feelings, sensations or ideas."

I notice, sitting opposite him, that I am feeling less defensive myself, less challenged and more inquisitive. The curiosity and the interaction suddenly have a gentler feel to them. Most importantly considering where we started, I feel more able to approach, make contact and make a fool of myself if necessary. His right lip can't help but smile a little.

The message here is not about changing the way you project your status, it is about identifying it and acting accordingly, with awareness. It is about understanding how unconscious high status can sometimes show up as arrogant, disinterested and overly intellectual. It is about how you can bring a gentle dissolution to the aspects that prevent contact between you and those you lead. (See Figure 38)

- What do you perceive to be the differences in status between you and the people around you?
- What are the unconscious symbols of status you may be projecting?
- How does this difference show up? How does it help?
- How does it limit your relationships? Where is it getting in the way of contact with others?
- What can you do to check your impact on others?
- What can you do to move from strong certainty to gentle uncertainty, discomfort, openness and accessibility?

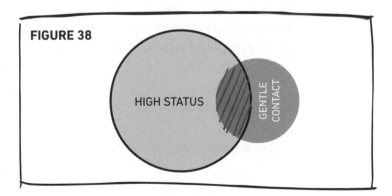

**FIGURE 38**

HIGH STATUS

GENTLE CONTACT

## THE EGO CHAMBER

The CFO has gone a little red in the face. He is tired because of the late nights and early mornings and working across the whole conference that is into its second day. He raises his voice to me, in exasperation.

"You knew what we were planning, you have had a couple of months to make any changes and now a couple of hours before they are to go on you are suggesting a new approach. No, we won't do it and will stick to what we planned."

The problem was that the presence of the senior leaders on stage during this conference had been desperately stage-managed; I was looking for some way, any way of ensuring they didn't look like a group of statues in this next session - to be able to demonstrate a different quality of listening to a business gathered in front of them;a business that had no belief in its own future.

The CFO had his set way of doing these things. A pretence at interaction by walking among the audience with a hand- held microphone, followed by a long set of slides that had a relentless quality to them. As gently as I could, I had dared to question this and do it in front of his peers.

A cold, slim smile preceded his next bruising statement.

"I haven't done many presentations in my career, yes, you must be right about the changes needed."

The rest of the executive team stand around in a semi-circle and shuffle their feet. No one looks at me. "Shit I have messed up again," I think.

"We will give them their questions in advance, they will have time to process the answers and no one will be surprised by what comes from the room. At. All. Now go and make it happen... please."

I duly did what I was told and cringed my way through the panel conversation - except it wasn't a conversation; it was a pre-prepared script with each of the actors delivering their lines in the agreed order. They sat uncomfortably on their comfortable sofas, fixed grins on their faces while they waited for the next question to be posed in exactly the order that had been pre-determined.

There was no tingle of the unexpected, daring or difficult. And they were delighted with the outcome. It was clean, went to plan, the HR director was lauded for his efforts and nothing changed, no one was touched, no one was inspired, no one had a view of anything other than the polish. It was an exercise in defence of senior egos.

The biggest opportunity missed in the situations described above is one of the audiences being heard, using them as a collective intelligence that has something critical to express. To use them as a way of amplifying voices that wouldn't normally be heard by the senior leaders sitting on that stage.

He takes to the stage in a very different way at the end of the conference. This is usually a time when loose ends are tied up and the leader makes sense of all that has gone on over the past few days. There is rousing applause and everyone leaves with a bounce in his or her step. But this wasn't what happened this time.

The thing that was different was the way in which he has been listening. It was as if he has placed himself outside of the conference or at least at the edges of it; quite different to being the driving force at the centre of it on whom all eyes are turned for the answer.

And in this last set piece of the conference it shows. It is as if he has been a reflective wall against which the voices of the past few days have bounced, but it is an intelligent wall that takes the voices, picks up even the quiet ones and finds a way of reflecting them back to the room with added force.

I watch for clues in his presence. In the conversation with the room there is something about his presence that welcomes the contact, invites people to go further than they thought they would, mirrors their emotion, person-by- person.

These are not pre-planned, conditioned cues and responses.

He is acting as an echo chamber, is there such a thing? If not there should be, I like the image it creates of how leaders of the Connected Age need to differentiate themselves from those of the Industrial Age. The leaders' role at the conference as echo chambers not ego chambers. (See Figure 39)

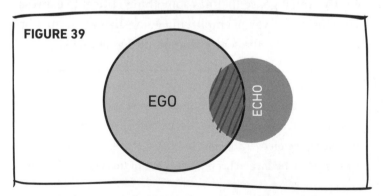

**FIGURE 39**

EGO ECHO

- What might it take from your ego to listen and echo in this way?

## START WITH A WHISPER

He is a softly-spoken man so many of the audience of 60 have to lean forward and crane their necks to catch everything he is saying. He is their new leader and they are keen to understand how to impress him... But he is confusing them so far.

They have spent two days in a poorly-ventilated hotel room not able to tell their teams what they were doing or why they would be absent. The faint Irish lilt continues for a while and then he asks them to get back to the office and implement all the changes they had talked about over the past two days.

This is a major change in strategic direction and one that will be a challenge to the existing ways of working. There is a range of reactions - complaints about the quality of our facilitation start to form on the tightly-pursed lips of a couple of the leaders; others turn to each other in bemusement looking for someone else to take a lead or ask another question, others rush to turn on their phones and return to the real work they had been missing. After what seems like a couple of hours but, in reality, was a couple of minutes, someone pipes up from the middle of the crowd.

"We don't have any materials to launch this initiative, are there some waiting for us?"
"No" says the leader
"Isn't it important that we all say the same thing though when we start talking to the business?"
"Sort of," says the leader.
"Is it ok if we produce our own materials for the implementation?"
"No," says the man of few words.
"No materials, no slides, no posters, just conversations."
"Let's do a series of roll out meetings which replicate the one we have just had then!"
"No. No meetings, no presentations, no pronouncements.

Nothing formal. No promises, no commitments. No shouting about what we intend."
"How will we communicate this then? We need some kind of engagement plan
from Communications or HR."

The Communications and HR people in the room shuffle their feet and look down
at the floor, suddenly captivated by the swirly brown carpet. I suspect it was more
of a burgundy shade at one time. I look down too, it reminds me of a carpet we had
in the hallway of our home when I was eight years old. I am lost for a moment in
a reverie, thinking back to that time and the cupboard under the stairs. I'm woken
up by his next request.

"Whisper it, whisper what we are about and what we intend to do. Keep it out of
the public domain for as long as we possibly can. We don't want anyone to know
about this before they have experienced the change we are talking about."

"You know that group won't be happy, we're unpicking something they have
committed to for a long time."

"I know but we have to believe what we are doing is best for our customers and
people. If anyone tries to stop you, find a way of circumventing him or her and
help each other to do so. We'll meet again in two weeks to share our progress and
learning. Good luck."

I have never forgotten this as a gentle approach to starting a
phase shift; in direct contrast to the proclamations and 'virtual
shouting' that goes on in most examples. It is almost a committed disinterest in generating a 'campaign', it trusts that, if the
business wants to hear and act, it will pick up on the whisper
and amplify it, in its own way and in its own time. The paradox
at play is that the speed and quality of engagement is usually

higher as a result and on the occasion that there is no response you waste less resource. (See Figure 40)

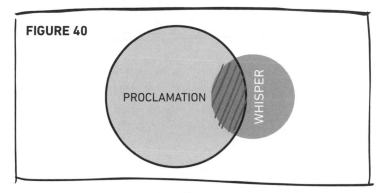

**FIGURE 40**

PROCLAMATION

WHISPER

Why do we need everyone to know about what we intend?

How much of this is connected to our ego needs for significance rather than what is best for the project in hand?

Whispering is a way of strengthening the container, a way of giving connections a chance to develop in support of what you put out there.

## IT MIGHT BE ME

There was a trend a few years ago, in the world of business conferences, to use the metaphor of music in its various guises as a source of learning for those leading complex businesses. I was involved in conference-after-conference with keynote speeches from famous conductors, or leaders learning how to conduct orchestras or jazz bands teaching the audience about how to improvise.

It was all interesting, entertaining and useful and, almost as quickly as it arrived, it disappeared with the conference organizers hungry for the 'next thing'. One particular experience from this time has stayed with me as a source of insight for those leading this complex transition we are in from one age to the next.

We are in a converted loft in Copenhagen, Denmark; wooden floors, metal girders and old factory windows give some clues to the manufacturing history of the site. This was abandoned long ago and it is now low-rent studio space for artists. I'm sure in 20 years' time it will be a location for future yuppies as is the way of these things.

We are sitting on hard, wooden benches without back- support, surrounding a classical quartet of musicians that has invited us to watch them rehearse. I think this time stood out from the crowd because we were here for the 'warts and all' rehearsal rather than the slick performance. There was a cellist; a flautist, a violinist and a viola player, who completed the four. They would play a passage (which sounded perfect to my ear) and then examine it together, letting us listen in on their conversation.

There were conversations about tempo and strength, tone and order, rhythm and musicality. Sometimes, we had to strain to hear what they were saying but we were rapt in our attention for the hour we watched them rehearse. Always wary of something artificial,I know this whole experience felt real to me as a spectator, rather than a prepared act of any kind. They were navigating a complex field.

They hadn't played together in this configuration before and were under a high degree of performance pressure. Most importantly, this was a first-time experiment for them as much as it was for us, it felt like the conditions were similar to a team in a business setting attempting a complex collaborative challenge for the first time.

We were given a few minutes to ask questions of the quartet. I was particularly struck by how gentle they were with each other in the examination of their performances. They didn't avoid pointing out each other's responsibilities and failings but there was a degree of polite interaction I hadn't been expecting, particularly after the tales I had heard of the drama that is often part of any artistic group endeavour. I asked them about this quality of interaction.

The cellist spoke first, describing the sensitivity he felt was necessary in any artistic group, as there was a strong overlap between the performance of the artist and their personal identity. So there was a gentle quality to the feedback, in recognition of how personally the recipient may take it. I understood that, and could see parallels for us, but it was the flautist's follow-up that stopped me in my tracks.

"I haven't thought much about this before but, for me, I think that if I am gentle in my feedback it is because it is a tentative thought. It is because the interactions between us, the tuning to each other's instruments, the creation of the sound between us...is all so relational and interconnected... that in the back of my mind there is always the suggestion that if something sounds off, it might be me."
(See Figure 41)

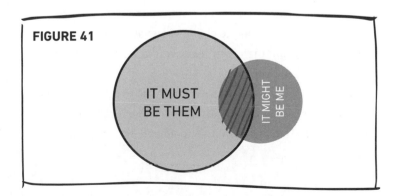

**FIGURE 41**

IT MUST BE THEM

IT MIGHT BE ME

# EIGHT (C)
## Practices for across us all

### CROSSING BORDERS

I am 17, tall, thin, with round glasses, wearing a white coat that used to be my father's old pharmacists' uniform and an ancient stethoscope wrapped around my neck. I am regularly mistaken for a doctor by the elderly patients on the ward but am employed as what used to be called an auxiliary nurse, the lowest of the untrained grades of nursing.

I am not here out of any vocational interest, purely selfish motives: to gain experience that would look good on my application to medical school and also to earn good money (for a student). My school friend's father has a nursing agency run out of a small, cramped, smoke-filled office that he shared with a hard-faced woman. The phones there are particularly loud and always ringing. The friendship meant they would often put me to the top of the list for the last-minute requests that came in when permanent members of hospital staff fell ill. If you were willing to change your plans at the last minute and work through the night then the money was good and I needed it.

Most of the other nurses treated the role I had in a transactional way. They were over-worked and under-resourced. I was there for one night, to do the work they didn't want to do or felt over-qualified to do and, in many cases, we would never meet again.

This night stands out in my memory as an experience of what it meant to be led by an elder. One of the patients on the ward had died, it was 2.30am, I was rubbing my bleary eyes and looking at my first cadaver. The ward was more silent than usual, or maybe I imagined it or maybe I blocked out the occasional moans of pain and cries for attention that usually accompanied a night shift.

"You haven't done this before, have you?" I thought, for a nanosecond, about bluffing, but one look at her face and I knew it was pointless.

"No. But just tell me what to do." Ever eager to please in those days.

"We are going to wash and prepare the body before the relatives see him."

"Ok."

"I will give you some materials and things in a minute but the most important part of this is how you think about the body in front of you."

"Huh?"

"Well, you could do what many of our colleagues do, treat it as an unpleasant job, the body as a piece of meat, get it over and done with as fast as possible."

"Understandable I guess."

"Or you could do the following. Imagine what you are about to do as the last act of kindness this man will ever receive and then act accordingly."

I wonder whether the transition we are in might have a gentle quality in the way it is facilitated between generations. For some reason, the role of our elders has become the focus of this section. How they stand between one age and another, helping us across the borders between the two. They don't know and we don't know what is coming next with any precision so what is needed is something more facilitative than directive; more kind than demanding.

## ELDER AND OLDER

They are members of the same peer group but you wouldn't know it if you spoke to them. Roughly the same age, they are nearing retirement and I have watched them over the past 20 years, sometimes close up sometimes from afar. I have listened to the stories about them around the organization and have occasionally seen them mentioned in the media for a great result or a crisis they were managing. They have had their supporters, their detractors, fans and sycophants, alter egos and nemeses. They are both readying to retire, I have been asked to support their last organizational transition, one will leave this organization as an older, the other as an elder.

The older looks older too. He walks slowly, with a slight hunch in his back, people have joked over the years that if he wasn't careful he might lean over too far and bang his head. His cough has become worse recently, although I notice it is often a substitute for saying something that feels unpalatable. I want to ask him what the cough is code for, what would he have said if the cough didn't get in the way.

Increasingly, he is treated as the elderly relative who must be cosseted from discomfort and, every now and then, he loses his temper and lashes out disproportionately. He knows his role is diminishing, his way of holding onto it for as long as possible is to put people down publicly, remind them he is still the boss until the day he walks out of there. He is holding on at any cost, I think scared of the loss of identity and purpose that will accompany retirement. In private, he expresses more and more cynicism about the organization, his treatment by the business. He is deeply self-involved and self-centred.

As he departs the organization, there is a lack of creativity and innovation in his unit. There is insufficient influence with business units outside his own; a vacuum of energy or 'thought leadership'; disagreement, that had been limited due to loyalty to him, now coming to the surface. Political tensions that were kept in check are heightening and now have a chance for greater expression; individuals who were insulated from a degree of adversity due to his protection now have to face it alone.

The elder still has a speed of movement that would impress if he were 10 years younger, a curiosity and twinkle that means he has remained engaged with developments and changes. This means that, as well as growing in status as he progressed, he also grew in his human presence, putting roots deep into the ground that continue to feed him, often out of sight of the day-to-day work. In the midst of difficulty, people still turn to him, not for direction but for wisdom; not for past detail but for a quality of cultural memory that is helpful. Particularly when moving from one age to another.

Our elders help us navigate between one age and another. The elders are there to keep the space strong and open while we learn what to do for ourselves. They are there, ready to step in when needed but just as ready to depart without their ego being bruised or in the way. They have a commitment to the future beyond themselves, beyond their physical death, which means they easily navigate the organizational death, which retirement triggers.

The older stands for himself; the elder stands for all of us. (See Figure 42)

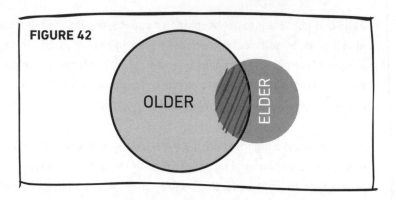

FIGURE 42

OLDER

ELDER

As you leave one stage and enter the next, the following questions may help you to do so as an 'Elder'.

You could even try them out as you leave one week and enter the next.

- Who are the people inside and outside the business who informed the leader you became?
- How did they touch you? What are you grateful for?
- How are you leaving this organization; better than when you joined it?
- What are your sources of pride? What have been the pivotal stories? What will be your legacy?
- Who, in your opinion, will struggle in some way as a result of your departure? With what can you leave them that may help?
- What do you want the organization to have learned as a result of your leadership? What is still left to pass on?
- How can you be of service as you leave and after you leave?
- What is the long-term commitment you want the business to hold onto through all of the short-term challenges?

## THE COMING HOME DINNER

We have just returned at the end of the day from a modern day 'hunt'. I have come to learn from the Native American people in Northern California about their ancient rituals and forms of development; ways of living together and working together that have been lost to the more modern societies we live in.

In the morning, we were tasked with navigating to a particular point in the high desert, collecting berries and bringing them back to the campsite by a particular time.

It was a long, hot, frustrating day. The landscape was fairly desolate, a combination of rocky paths, juniper bushes and a kind of pine tree local to the area with much sharper needles than the ones I recall at home. We had been given water, basic self-care and navigation advice and were left to get on with it. They called this process 'coyote mentoring'.

On our return, we were glad to see the part of the road that indicated the camp was at the other end. It looked so different in the light of dusk to how it had in the light of dawn, we thought we had missed it. Our speed picked up a little and we crossed the camp threshold to find most of the other groups already back and waiting on a couple of stragglers.

The facilitators in the camp had spent the day preparing food for our return, everything was laid out ready and we sat around the camp circle, thankful that the usual evening chores weren't waiting for us. There was something about the spirit of service demonstrated in the preparation of the meal that was particularly touching.

But we had relaxed too soon. The second half of our test was only just beginning. Over the meal, we were asked a series of questions that showed to me how little I had actually achieved on the hunt.

An important contribution had been made in terms of the berries found, picked and returned to the tribe but there were so many other questions to which we struggled to provide a meaningful answer.

Having been involved in 'outward bounds' work many years previously, I was half expecting an examination of how the team performed under stress; I had mentally prepared for the questions but they didn't come.

- Where were the biggest berries?
- What was the soil condition like?
- What was the water condition like?
- Who else had been on the site?
- Who else did you meet on the way? Where were they heading?
- Which animals, birds and insects did you see?
- What were the places for shelter or shade on your route?
- If you didn't have a map how would you find your way back?
- What were your navigation markers?

After stumbling through the questions we were offered other processes that helped us access a lot of learning that wasn't immediately accessible; journaling, meditative processes, imagination exercises, storytelling as memory, peer conversations and others.

The facilitators explained that this analysis served two purposes, one for the individual hunters who were being encouraged to a level of reflection that opened up different areas of learning. The second purpose was that the whole community benefited from the hunters' individual exploration as much as they did the food.

As we set out to explore the unknown territories ahead of us, or ask others to do so on our behalf, it struck me that this 'coyote mentoring' form could be very useful. We could become as interested in what people learned on the way to and from their destination as we were in their reaching it. This could result in learning for the whole community, not just ourselves as individuals.

# NINE

## Persistence

— – — - — - — - — — - — – — - —

You seem to want accepting defeat to lead to a brighter future. Perhaps. What is the energy of defeat? Or the energies of defeat? Certainly giving up something 'past its sell by' can be a releasing and energetic process … but I don't think always. Could be a quietening or some other quality too.

Final thought, is there enough in this book about the invisible companionship you talk about? I feel that increasing the reader's faith and belief that there are others out there who share their ambition and feeling, is critical to them finding the courage to live in the age of connection! Not sure how you do this but maybe it needs more space in the book.

— – — - — - — - — — - — – — - —

# NINE (A)
## Practices for inside myself

## A LIST OF 36 WAYS TO KEEP IT SIMPLE

We are preparing as a team for some work at a conference the following day. One of our team members has gone ahead and is reporting back from the venue where he has spent the day with the client.

"A few notes from today which I hope will be helpful for tomorrow: we are in a nice room, which is too big for the number of people gathered. Only about two-thirds of those who were supposed to come along actually did. Tomorrow, we will probably have about the same number, at most, although there will be some people tomorrow who weren't there today.

The atmosphere was dull, quiet and serious. Presentations were dull, quiet and serious - lots and lots of initiatives, numbers, words, but no sense of cohesion or overall meaning; no attempt to stimulate conversation or engagement. It felt like the organization at its lowest ebb, everyone desperately trying to convince themselves that the new plan made sense, but knowing the world was moving on very fast and ignoring the plan.

There was talk of integration with the new business-exhausted people (their words). The new CEO arrived earlier this year from one of their competitors, started a big strategic review which led to lots of new initiatives and job shuffling. Whether you are viewed as 'core' or 'non-core' to the group now seems to be determined by your potential profit margin - meaning that some who were previously side-lined are now in the spotlight and vice versa. People in the acquired business are worried about being consumed by the parent company (employee satisfaction and customer satisfaction have both fallen).There is a number of paradoxes in play but no one sees them as such, or if they do they are not willing to talk about them.

- A strategic pillar of simplicity and eight (I kid you not) simplicity programmes, plus countless other initiatives, strategic themes and sub-themes
- A strategic intent of focusing on the customer relationships and decisions, which are based (it seems to me) entirely on profit and product
- A very tired organization and "no sympathy for tiredness" in the executive team
- A desire for people to be passionate and to up the pace alongside stunningly unexciting leadership (if today was any indication)
- A need to collaborate much more effectively and yet make no time for conversations
- A strategic theme about becoming a trusted advisor and "... client contract amendments are a great opportunity to build in profit"

Some data points for you that blew my mind: 16 major change initiatives (considered a big step change in simplification); 1,100 unique internal reports; 255,000 pages of analysis; 400 key performance indicators, produced every month; 12 divisions within this part of the organization (considered a huge streamlining of the previous organizational structure).
See you tomorrow. Looking forward to it!"

When faced with this quality of environment, one that is common in our large organizations, it is easy and understandable that many choose to give up.

Some give up obviously, through leaving organizational life; others less obviously through keeping their job but deciding to give as little of themselves as possible, resigned to their lack of efficacy in a system too hard to change.

So, the final quality we are covering in our exploration of power and love is that of persistence as a form of power. I have struggled to find the right word for this quality as I don't want it collapsed with its near enemy - that of endurance. This quality is not about enduring the inevitable pain and exhaustion of a long distance runner. It is about developing ourselves to live through the difficulty of what we are attempting.

Those of us 20 years into our careers have chosen a difficult time in which to lead our large organizations - the disorientating, often unrewarding liminal phase in the middle of a phase shift. This time doesn't offer any degree of resolution; this is its poignancy. There is no immediate resolution, you don't necessarily get to move on from this and I have no idea for how long we will be here.

So, learning to lead with persistence, despite a lack of resolution, becomes an important quality. In this chapter, we are talking about persistence in our acknowledgement of defeat; persistence in our capacity to keep feeling; persistence in wiggling through the restrictions in whatever way we can create; persistence in developing practices that keep us sharp and healthy; persistence in staying open and connected in the face of old systems that nudge us towards closing down and disconnecting.

## GIVING UP THE FIGHT

"I have never missed plan two years in a row so if it happens this year that is the end of the road for me."

"Does that mean they will fire you?"

"No it means I will resign and find something else to do."

There is a range of expression on the faces of members of this team as I look around the room; mostly dazed, if not shocked. They are all struggling to find a way to meet the new targets and weren't expecting this from their leader.

The usual response would have been a shouting match. In would come the boss, grim-faced with little time for pleasantries. A pretence of going through the agenda would be acted out until some random item would become an excuse for the trading of accusations and aggression. One member of the team described this response as combative. That was my sense too.

Each meeting was a test - would you end up top dog or bottom of the pile in this exchange? There would be emotional and tactical preparation before the meeting to ensure the former and emotional recovery and tactical panic if it turned out you were the latter. It sapped energy from everyone in the team and when you have been in this position for a while it shows on your face, even if you think you are doing a good job of hiding it: stern, still, staring faces, statues for bodies, tensed and waiting for the next accusation, hyperactive minds working out every permutation.

This was the first time he had publicly looked inward rather than outward when looking for a place to lay responsibility and blame.

"I have tried everything I know how to do, everything that has worked for me in the past, but, if anything, it is making things worse rather than better. My holiday has helped, it is the first time I have been away from work for three weeks and even that decision was telling me something was wrong on the inside rather than just the outside. And then I received the 360° feedback results which some of you completed. Thank you. They were a shock to me. I just don't know what to do now; I feel this team, this business slipping away from me. If I am going to go down, I want to go down fighting. That was my first thought and then something else came to mind: maybe the fighting is the problem, fighting to hold on to a way of leading this team. It is what I know to do but it is not working and it is out of date."

There is nothing wrong with defeat; I often secretly wish it for our clients, just enough failure so that a significant re-evaluation becomes necessary. There is a paradoxical strength in this kind of giving up; accepting defeat makes our longer-term persistence more sustainable. (See Figure 43)

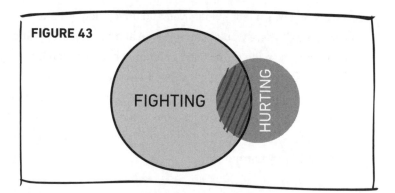

**FIGURE 43**

FIGHTING   HURTING

## TOUCHING DEFEAT

I am sitting in the small room my supervisor uses to examine my work. She is old, the sofa always creaks when I sit down, the door doesn't shut properly, it is comforting in its disorder. The books are piled a little higher today on the coffee table. I always expect them to topple over but they never do, it will be some kind of sign when they eventually succumb.

The nights are drawing in, I am tired, irritable, cold and it is only Monday. We start talking about my work, particularly one of the projects I would like to hide from her examination. As I become more experienced, it is easier to hide behind my supposed knowledge but I know I have to push this particular difficulty into the light.

Looking back on this project, it should have been obvious from the start that it was going to defeat us. My story was that the group structure was too oppressive, the CEO too invested in its image, the executive team antagonistic to anything that challenged the status quo and leading a business that had been repeatedly disappointed by previous broken promises.

"We really want to shake things up," they would say and then react negatively and punitively to the initial stirrings of difference. Our team would be returned to a never-ending round of justification for something the business wasn't ready for yet. But my ego got the better of me; if anyone could help this organization, we could. The business played a critical role in our society, the people in it were deeply committed, doing their best, and the venture's success was a marker of our ability as an economy and country. But now it had become too heavy a weight, one with which I didn't have enough support.

Usually, this process of supervision generates new insight, a way of viewing the situation that I hadn't considered. It renews my energy and off I go, bouncing back into the fray with a vitality to which others contribute. This time, it didn't and I left feeling worse. I returned the following week, and the next one, with the same outcome, expending more energy with less return.

Defeat is not something we allow ourselves to talk much about is it? Well, sometimes we do but it is in a way that immediately returns us to success, you know... the cliché that my failures taught me a lot and prepared me for my future successes. There is nothing wrong with that version of events, I love a good cliché and have trotted it out enough times in my past. And at the same time, I am curious about a new quality surfacing from many of our clients, one that we struggle, in the day-to-day conversations, to describe, to share and to integrate into our ways of working and our challenge to the status quo.

"Sounds like you are defeated by this", says the supervisor.
I feel my internal world crumble, I don't do defeat. Much of my psychology and the underpinning structure of my belief system is that we "don't do defeat". There is always a way through – isn't there? Experience has taught us (and many of those we support) that this is nonsense. If we only identify with our potency, we are missing a whole part of ourselves that wants to understand defeat and let ourselves sink into it.

In the supervision, I turn inwards into my body and realise my arms feel weightless, like jelly, and that there is nothing there. "Push against my hand," says my supervisor. I am 6'3" tall, and while a long way from being Arnold Schwarzenegger should have been able to push over this elderly woman with three fingers of one hand.Right now, I can hardly lift my arms and pushing seems out of the question. So much of my life has been spent avoiding defeat that to allow it a place is something new.

When I fully accept it as part of our connected life then, in that moment of acceptance, real acceptance, something shifts. What did move? I can't describe it vividly enough, I just know something did.

What I would say to myself now is "don't get cut off from the defeated part of yourself. When you do, you freeze. And so do all those who are relying on your leadership."

Defeat is mostly avoided or hidden in the Industrial Age as a source of shame. In the Age of Connection we may become more used to its repeating nature, maybe even welcoming of it.

Colleagues and clients have described it as: "Nothing changes until someone says we have had enough, we can't do this anymore, is this all there is? When you feel that deeply enough you know that something new and positive will emerge but it comes from a place of giving up rather than battling through."

"Our institutions often suck the life and energy out of something that was once alive. But we earn the right to start something new by allowing what needs to die to die. This includes brands, strategies, ideas, structures, promotions, and career expectations. In keeping it all going we have lost the ability to live with the reality of what is in front of us. It is becoming an unnatural way of operating."

So maybe the Industrial Age leader refuses to accept defeat under any circumstance, holding on to a belief, against all the evidence, that we will overcome. The energy is invested in the fight and there is desperation to avoid defeat. Another version of this may be those who are so exhausted and defeated that they give up on everything - themselves, their colleagues, the business, their whole cause. They leave corporate life, or their organization, with some resentment and a lot of disappointment in themselves and others. Their pessimism takes hold in such a way that they can't shake loose from it.

Maybe the leader in the Age of Connection touches defeat, feels it deeply and then finds a way of integrating it into their work. It gives them a lighter touch somehow. They are not carrying the same weight of expectation in themselves. You can cross this particular threshold through your compassion for defeat in yourself and others.

As we end this section you might want to ask yourself "what am I finished with?"

Declare it to as many people around you as you feel comfortable and see what emerges afterwards.

# NINE (B)
## Practices for between us

### THE NEVER-ENDING CURVE

There are 200 employees, standing on a line that initially expresses a change curve. It has been hastily prepared by fixing thick masking tape to the carpet of this large, slightly gloomy, hotel conference room. I have a faint memory of having been here for another event one evening; it didn't scrub up that well then either. They stand along a line that starts to decline and then slumps into a crevasse and then slowly recovers ending at a point higher than where it started.

The 200 people are part of an engineering company that has lost its way over the past few years. They have a young age profile, having been recruited for a customer service-type role that was new for the business. But the business is rejecting change and this unit has gone through three directors in the past 15 months, has had some internal investigations conducted and is suffering from a high level of staff turnover.

There is a range of clothing styles on display, many of which I am too old to recognize let alone attempt to match. Some carry the style with panache, most look a tad uncomfortable in the tightness and high heels of it all, as they stand on the line looking to their right and left. Some large groups huddle together, shoulders touching, others spread out until at the ends of the curve in which they are standing in ones and twos.

What is different this time is the stages that have been defined and named on the curve: numb, cynical, discouraged, disorientated, scared, curious, hopeful, energetic, committed and achieving.

They have created their own labels to represent how they have felt and it strikes me we now have a change curve for those bringing the novel to bear.

From their positions, they tell their stories; the thing that hits me most strongly is how frequent and quick the movements between stages are. They don't follow the usual pattern of a change curve though; there is no progression to an end point. The group is in a constant state of flux and this becomes the key insight for them and for me. If we are standing at the edges of the Industrial Age, attempting to bring forth something novel, then there is going to be a constant shifting between positions, many of them difficult and all of them, including the ones associated with success don't last long.

The group decides to pick up the masking tape so they can turn a curve into a circle; it means there is no end point and you can start anywhere: start energetic, end up numb; start disorientated, end up hopeful.

The next little bit of magic that takes place during the conversations that follow is yielded simply by more contact and connection. Even those who had felt themselves rooted to a particular position found that, by making more contact, they moved, even if it was just a small way to another position on the curve (now circle). Contact and connection is the way out of the stickiness - contact with the organizational family, friends, old beliefs, renewed belief, your own humanity and other people's stories.

The circle takes on a different symbolism for the 200 in their ongoing recovery from difficulty, they agree to meet regularly as a large group and make contact with where they are, each time taking up their positions in the circle and speaking from that place without judgement or fear. It becomes a virtual gathering 'around the campfire' where the battle-weary can recuperate, create their myths and sharpen their swords before returning to the fray.

In the Connected Age we need to allow ourselves to feel and to allow ourselves to do so together. There is nothing to be done in the most turbulent times other than feel our way through and yet that is the very thing we often stop ourselves doing. It seems far easier to get on with the work in hand or create a drama about the situation. But a departure, or any other ending, without feeling suggests there was no intimacy in the first place; that we have not invested our whole selves in the work. We only invested the part of ourselves that is a machine and so the ending is simply a case of switching off that part of ourselves and going home for our supper. (See Figure 44)

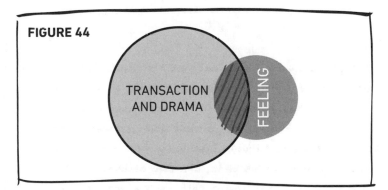

**FIGURE 44**

TRANSACTION AND DRAMA

FEELING

- Can you think of all the things that are ending now in your work life?
- How do you defend against 'feeling' their ending?
- What would it be like to just let all the feelings come,

what is the fear that holds you back?
- Name all the feelings, write them down if you want to, but then go back and feel them; naming, capturing, writing is different to feeling.
- Now try saying them out loud starting with 'I feel....'
- How might you gather people together for a conversation about this?

I know, I know, I'm sorry; this is starting to sound like some kind of self-help manual for the emotionally-repressed in the Industrial Age.

Maybe it is self-help, and if that is what one of the reviews says, maybe it is no bad thing.

Don't be put off by cringing, just have a go and see what happens.

## HAND, BUCKET, WATER

He puts down the phone at home and catches his reflection in the mirror: slightly dazed with an inane, fixed smile on his face. One member of his team has just handed in their resignation, it came out of the blue, he thought things were going so well – or at least better than they had been. Just before Christmas, he had seen this team member at his best, the two of them held a meeting with an important client and it felt as if a corner had been turned. Then, two months later, there was the resignation.

In the days that followed, he experienced a range of emotions that began with an initial state of what he thought was acceptance. "Yes of course you must go," he said, having heard the rationale for the departure. "It makes a lot of sense, I think it is the right thing to do, both for you as an individual and for us as an organization." They talked more about how it had come to this point and then moved on to the work to be done: "We'll work it out so there is a smooth transition here." There was goodwill on both sides, and it would be done well: "We need to manage all of this with your stakeholders in the business and plan your transition, we want to make sure you leave with the best chance of success in your next role."

However, at the team meeting a few days later, he was saying the same sort of thing when, all of a sudden, other stuff started coming out. There was a small opportunity to punish the leaver, an issue of detail over a current project that wasn't up to scratch, and he took it. It was messy, clumsy, ineffective and dramatic and others in the team started to react to what they were seeing and hearing. Then the conversation was shut down quickly as they needed to move on to the next agenda item.

There is an oft-quoted metaphor in our line of work that says "a person leaving an organization is like a hand being removed from a bucket of water". The instant the hand is removed, the water closes over the space and it is as if there had never been anyone there. There is the part of me that belongs to Industrial Age organizations that can relate to this. It is also a powerful way of defending against the thought that we may have invested emotion in our work. I don't believe this holds true where we have worked in real communities and developed an intimacy of relationship. It won't hold true in the Age of Connection, the container needs something different.

## WHY THIS, WHY ME, WHY NOW?

I have just finished my pain au chocolat in a hurry, jamming the last piece into my mouth and chewing fast so I can answer the phone before it reaches the eighth ring and goes to voicemail. I leave the noisy cafe and step into the cold pedestrian area outside it, pulling on my winter coat as I go. It is one of my colleagues, he is responsible for a significant competitive pitch the following day for a recently-merged organization. What this business requires is very much within our area of expertise and we are all excited by the prospect of the work.

What I hear on the other end of the line is a voice full of anxiety, describing a series of difficulties, misunderstandings and mishaps that have led to neither member of the two-person team doing the pitch being able to attend. I am scrolling through my diary on the phone. Ok, I can move some things around and go in their place, I will have to beg the forgiveness of those I am letting down. It starts in less than 24 hours, it is more than 200 miles away, and I have no understanding of the pitch or any relationship with the prospective clients.

Somehow, and somewhat unexpectedly, what comes out of my mouth in response to the story is: "How exciting"! It is the first time I have experienced this response. Typically, I would have been particularly concerned with finding out how on earth we had ended up in this situation and confirming just how difficult it was going to be to do anything about it.

"Why is he unwell now?"
"What will the client expect?"
"Is there any point?"
"How on earth will we schedule the other work I would have to move?"
"Why does it have to be so far away?"
"Why this? Why me? Why now?"

You can ask the same questions with a very different mindset. In the Industrial Age we would be asking them with a view to persecution, victim-hood and complaint. Answers that build defences and reduce potential vulnerability, answers that explain how we got here and who is responsible.

In the Age of Connection we may have to get used to these situations cropping up much more regularly. What will come of this? What is the mystery with which we can engage? What will we learn? What is the chance to build or deepen another connection? What is being tested? (See Figure 45)

This is a mystery with which to engage and a call to adventure. I don't mean this as a pretence, self-hypnosis or deceit - I mean it as a way of working to which we will all relate positively in the future. Those of you already great at 'winging it', and suffering from a perception that you are doing it because you are lazy, rejoice! Your time has come.

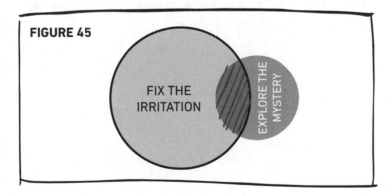

**FIGURE 45**

FIX THE IRRITATION

EXPLORE THE MYSTERY

## WORKING WITH OUR RELUCTANCE

We are playing a game. It comes from the world of theatre but we are using it here to help understand the dynamics in a team that defaults to something particularly 'bi-polar'. The leader moves to make something happen, the team opposes. The team moves to make something happen, the leader opposes. I am exhausted just dipping into this dynamic from time-to-time; I can't imagine how tiring it must be to be in it permanently.

I am reminded of an old cycle that starts with stillness and ends with completion and letting go. In between, there is connection and action. Here there is connection of sorts, lots of action but it doesn't go anywhere, no completion, no letting go, no stillness. The result is a team stuck, lacking creativity or cut through, deeply frustrated or (in the event that something is forced through) resentful.

So the game goes like this: we play it in pairs; person A makes an imaginary suggestion accompanied by actions, person B follows that suggestion saying "yes, let's!" until they determine, for some reason, that they don't want to say yes anymore and say "no".

"Let's go for a walk!"
"Yes, let's!"
"Let's follow this path down to the beach."
"Yes, let's!"
"Let's take off our shoes and socks!"
"Yes, let's!"
"Let's go for a paddle."

At the point that person B says "No", person A has to respond with "OK, so what comes next?" Which means the responsibility for suggestions rests with person B.

"No."

"Ok so what comes next?"

"Let's go and buy some ice cream."

"Yes let's!"

Repeat ad infinitum.

The game, in itself, is a lot of fun and there is a magic ingredient. When you say "no" or "ok, what comes next?" you have to say it with a smile on your face. It changes the whole dynamic. Try it out in any situation, at home or work, you will see what I mean. It is such a simple challenge to the habit of accompanying every "no" with a frown or stern face. That is what we do in the Industrial Age isn't it?

The power of a "no" back then was a full stop to something, usually quite a stern one. And it stopped the energy flowing through the people, through the idea, through the organization, through the market. I am not suggesting for a moment that we say "yes" to everything, but I am suggesting that, in order to stay connected and flowing in the next age, we accompany our "no" with a smile and an "ok, what comes next?"

A few weeks later we are together again, this time in a business meeting. It is a difficult moment, a presentation has just finished, the tension is palpable, and she has got it completely wrong, I think. Her proposal, in response to the customer situation, is poorly thought through and had little impact. And then she surprises us all and we learn something about moving gently with pace. When everyone says "no", she doesn't justify it, defend it, and make the other party wrong she just says, "Ok so what comes next?" with a smile on her face.

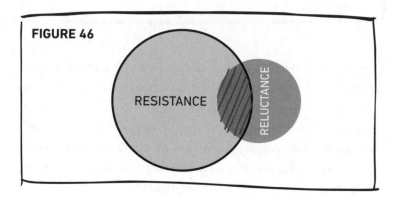

**FIGURE 46**

If we conceptualize a "no" as resistance in the Industrial Age it means, in our leadership response, that 'they' have to be overcome. (See Figure 46)

If we conceptualize a "no" as reluctance in the Connected Age it means they don't understand yet or do understand and don't want to play. Or they have some other priorities that mean they can't attend to this immediately. "Ok, what comes next?" can keep us going with heart and a lightness of touch.

# NINE (C)
## Practices for across us all

OFF THE GRID [8]

*"Working for a large global company, as I do, has its pros and cons. On the one hand, you get to interact with as many smart people as you could possibly imagine, you have the resources to get things done and, above all, there is a good chance of doing things that really matter, like solving problems for big customers; even, occasionally, changing the world for the better. On the other hand, mostly, due to our sheer size, we have a large number of policies telling us what we can do.*

Often the policies are helpful, explaining how to do what you want to do while staying out of trouble. It would be impossible to operate without them in such a large organization. Yet, the longer I am here, the more I have begun to feel their limitations, to the point where they can become stifling showstoppers if you let them.

It would be very easy for me to hide behind the rules. No one could criticize me for doing so, but I know I just couldn't get the things done that I needed to do. So, having spent the early part of my career learning the rules and understanding them, I have spent the latter part learning how to break the rules responsibly when I feel I need to.

For example, in my role as a research architect, it is crucial to gain early feedback from customers on the value of the solutions we develop. This involves lots of early-stage demos at customer events, as well as spreading the word through various means, including social networks.

It became apparent that one of the best ways of doing this was by posting short, compelling videos on the web. The official policy requires me to gain approval from the global communications team before making a video available publicly.

Some of the feedback I have received after submitting videos for approval have ranged from requests to "remove the Firefox logo from the demo of a web application", (which would entail a huge amount of additional work), to "asking Google for permission to use their logo in a Google Maps product", (which would slow down our progress to an absolute crawl).

I am frequently left with a choice - to follow the advice, stay absolutely legally safe and make no progress, or ignore it and take some risk. My decision has been to take the risk. I have produced many videos; I blog; I share frequently on Twitter; and the best thing is that I still work here.

On one occasion, someone from the department setting the policy reached out to me and - in a friendly way - informed me that my ignoring policy rules could get me fired. My only response was that, if the company decided to fire me for what I was doing, then it was the wrong company for me to work for anyway so I was fine with it. At that point, I realised it is too convenient to use 'business risk' as a reason for not innovating, whereas it is actually the risk to ourselves that we are not willing to accept. I fully accept the risk to myself and I delight in finding new ways to develop great products quickly whether or not I break the rules."

This is a common story among those determined not to be defeated by the restrictions of the Industrial Age culture in which they are operating. The Challenger in me loves hearing them and being part of them and, at the same time, there is a new version of them emerging. It is one that benefits from the same spirit of persistence, but does it in a way that finds and builds connection.

## WIGGLING TO INDEPENDENCE

It was dead, the orders from corporate headquarters were clear; the project was dead in the water. It was as clear as the rather curt email he had in front of him, printed out on a piece of paper. For some reason, he still printed certain emails, maybe it wasn't quite believable until he held the paper in his hand.

We had all been at the launch at an excellent, media-friendly venue in town, with just enough 'razzmatazz', without overdoing it in this age of austerity. Would anyone there have believed him if he said, just two weeks later, that the project was no more?

So, in his own way, with a grim determination and not very much thought, he chose not to listen and to do what he thought was necessary. He believed in this product, it had everything that was needed to compete more fully with the dominant competitor and every instinct he had, informed by years of working in this industry, said not to stop now.

He started writing, it didn't take much thought, just allowing the keyboard to spew out what he believed. There wasn't much on the paper in the way of numbers but plenty of faith and as he sat back after 20 minutes of pounding away on the tired keyboard, he saw it for what it was. A manifesto, a call to gather across the whole organization, from whichever discipline you hailed, if you wanted to keep going. It was an exercise in engaging his imagination rather than his business school education.

He typed in a few names he knew would share his opinion and pressed send. Two days later, as he waded through emails, he started to notice responses from people who weren't on the original distribution list and felt a flutter of fear inside. What had he done? This would be just the thing to get him fired after all these years of solid service.

And then, about half-way through the list, there was a mail that said an independent discussion forum had been set up, outside of the organization's formal mechanisms: if you were interested in the initiative, please join the conversation.

During the forum, magic had started to happen. Maybe it was just that something was needed after all the lay-offs and disappointments, colleagues leaving, competitors succeeding, promotions delayed and bonuses reduced. People needed something that wasn't about 'death by a thousand cuts', but about a source of new life. There were connections being made between all parts of the globe, initiatives that he had never heard of, individuals with highly-specialist jobs talking to others in other specialisms.

There was a life here beyond the silos and selfishness that dominated the day-to-day formal culture. It was more curious, challenging, there was belief, hope and ambition. Most of all, in the face of being told "no", there was determination to carry on regardless. Together, they cobbled together resources from a range of budgets and bought an exhibition space at the global conference. They were going to take the next stage of their work there and see what their customers thought of it.

I asked him afterwards how he summarized what happened here.

"I think I realise now that when there is nowhere for my insights and energy to go, if they are blocked by the organization, I kind of 'wiggle' my way to independence. That first time, I just acted and wasn't sure what was happening, now I do it a bit more deliberately, it keeps me connected to my hope even when the situation may look hopeless."

These 'wiggling', connected local efforts are wonderfully resilient. The thing that stands out about this new way of operating in the Age of Connection is the way it taps into already existing communities of interest and passion. It is tempting to believe, in the new age, that you have to build new communities before you can do anything meaningful. Another way of thinking may simply be that the community you need already exists and your role is to recognize it so that it can be found. (See Figure 47)

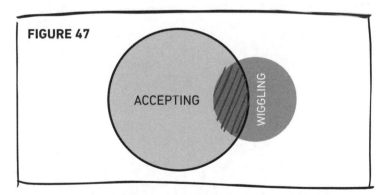

**FIGURE 47**

ACCEPTING

WIGGLING

They typically gather around initiatives, processes or solutions that cut across functional boundaries. Search for those that have been fighting for a cause without hierarchy to back them up, they are your starting point. They are counting more on their passion and persistence as a source of power than their organizational position.

Those who are beginning to operate in this way are not look-ing to destroy the hierarchy of the Industrial Age; this will change in its own time. While they wait, they find and devel-op communities that can act as a lubricating force, rendering the hierarchy more persistent, fluid, flexible and purposeful in the face of change. (See Figure 48)

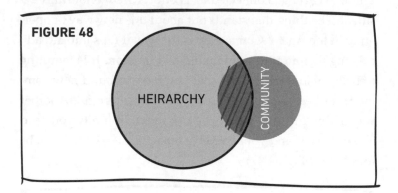

**FIGURE 48**

HEIRARCHY

COMMUNITY

# TEN

## Telling your own story

— – — - — - — - — - — - — - —

"The book is a melee. So many strands that it ought not to be pulled together in such a trite unfulfilling conclusion. I admit that not all the book has touched me that well but it is different!

You have exhausted your persistence and really just written another chapter with a final page that tries to consolidate what you have already weaved us through. This is not really a conclusion, and definitely not one that leaves the reader energized and wanting to know more, or more importantly do more and try more. So my question to you is 'OK, what comes next?'

As I expected, you kept me waiting until the very end, until chapter ten, to snap everything into focus. It was like having my mind see the set of toppled dominos that are all the previous chapters, suddenly stand up and come to order and meaning.

You have taken me on a long walk through the worlds of organizations and I have seen, like a fly on the wall, sometimes painfully, sometimes depressingly, sometimes encouragingly, right into their souls in technicolor.

— – — - — - — - — - — - — - —

The following pages make up a summary of sorts although I would rather you skipped this part and formed your own conclusions and interpretations. Those interested in my attempt to pull together the various strands might want to read it but it is just one interpretation.

## GIVING UP CONTROL

The market is shrinking. The competition is hotting up. Conversations go round-and-round in circles and the reports of the drubbings they are taking from the CEO increase. The recent set of values agreed and enacted are in shreds on the floors of the meeting rooms that still display the posters.

He hits the table with his hand: "This is what I want, what is going wrong. I want high achievers, high energy, pride, a can-do spirit, hunger, restlessness, agitating and refreshing our business. What I have is technical brilliance and experts on how to manage quality, safety and budget cuts."

The industry forces are dramatic, no artificial enhancements are needed on the PowerPoint graphs that go up one after the other; traffic on the network is increasing exponentially, costs of providing the network and maintaining it are not far behind. Revenues are flattening over the same time period. The 'easy' cost-savings had been actioned over the past three years, now where would they turn?

They have eeked out four or five percentage points of profit growth over the past three years; mostly from the bottom line and a point or two from the top line for good measure. The analysts are happy enough but the profit growth doesn't tell anything like the full story.

There is a quiet young man in the back of the room. In the silence after the table-banging, he offers an answer but his voice is too timid to be heard. "We have to give up control," he says.

I seek him out afterwards; he was young enough to see something but no one else in the room was. The response of the senior executives to the situation was to take more control not less: more data, more measures, more projects, more project names that start with superlatives, more price rises, more pressure on suppliers, more auditing, more mechanical stuff.

"Our future lies in a way of working that they can't live with," he said. "Everything today is so slow and what we are doing to address the problem is slowing us down even more. The CEO is right, in a way - our culture is a massive part of this, but he has also helped create it. We have so many products, literally thousands of plans, high complexity in the way we have to hold, and relate to, our customers.

This complexity feeds the machine, keeps hierarchies and structures in place but doesn't give us what we need. Our work is constrained by our organizational design. When we manage to bring new innovations to market, it is a turgid process with a high risk of something going wrong post-launch. The stack of IT projects we need to help us grows bigger and bigger but, with so many interfaces, no project receives the commitment it needs and ends up being compromised... so the stack has to grow again. The projects that aren't satisfied put in place workarounds that bring more complexity and slow us down further."

It is the next piece that hits me hard as he says it. This is the heart of why we are doing the work we are doing.

"We believe that the more we control things the more money we will make. But we won't. Our growth will only come through less control. Less control equals growth. It is what our customers want from us but we don't trust ourselves to deliver in that environment."

The need for a change in our Industrial Age organizations is coming under increasing pressure from the ultimate arbiters: our customers and our workforces. Customers want to be users of what we sell but they also want to be creators, contributors, peers and producers. They are ready to resist the more passive relationships of the past where intelligence was supposedly centralized in the organization and the willing, passive followers were consumers, audiences, listeners, buyers of a polished strategy, product or message that was handed down to them.

This scenario assumes there is a challenge to the dominant cultural meme in organizational life, one that has been in place for two hundred years - that of management control as the primary organizing force.

In the ordered domains that characterized the Industrial Age, only some people knew the answers. They would be relied on to investigate, analyze the problem and respond to it.

Many executives and senior managers sense the challenges to the power and status relationships that are starting to emerge. Perhaps the biggest problem they are facing is that the end of control is equated in their minds with the end of growth.

Their control of information, resources, regulation, people and finance is under threat. The future is arriving quickly and confusing them. Structures and cultures are creaking under the strain of a workforce that wants to have flows of information and energy converted quickly into useful just-in-time knowledge and understanding. We have a workforce that knows problem-solving is more effective through its enhanced internal and external networks than waiting for decision-making from 'on high'.

In the Connected Age, we are becoming more familiar with disordered domains that cannot be managed in the same way because they are complex processes, evolving dynamically in real time. No sooner have we analyzed them and decided what to do, than they have changed again. In this complex environment we're basically systematically 'winging it', seeing what works and what doesn't.

So many large organizations that have failed recently, (some while they were our clients), have tipped themselves into a chaotic decline in performance because they insisted on acting as if they were in a highly-ordered environment when they were not. The executives and advisors all colluded in some kind of major fantasy; that they were operating in an ordered environment that allowed them to manage their organizations in a distant, industrial and disconnected manner.

We considered, in the first part of this book, some of the consequences of maintaining or furthering this degree of disconnection. I am not saying it is always like this but we have experienced too many of these environments not to accept that they persist. At their worst, people we care about inside these places have described themselves as lonely, isolated, despairing, numb, irresponsible, afraid, hopeless, abusive, cold, hyper-cognitive, exhausted, unethical, dull, habitual, defended, closed, repetitive, mechanical, controlling, hyper-efficient, unresponsive, tight, constrained, paranoid, destructive. That's a tough read and we find it hard to live with the consequences of this environment on those we love. And, of course, it is a testament to their spirit that, despite the tough conditions, many of them are somehow retaining their creativity, energy, success, relationships, balance and good humour!

In the middle section of the book we saw that, if we are serious about shifting this way of being, it may be a soul-wrenching experience for us all. Something is ending and before we can rush to the next beginning there is some psychological and emotional work to do in the middle. It is particularly hard because it is never a clean break. In this middle, liminal phase there is plenty of conflict inside us and between ourselves; we become an expression of that conflict in our day to day. This is a conflict between two phases, neither of which is fully resolved, one in its ending and another in its beginning.

The last part of the book concentrated on four practices to which we dedicate ourselves in the Age of Connection. They are rooted in the belief that executive power in the future comes from developing the relationships and connections across all people in an organizational setting. The deeper the connections are, the quicker a business can access and harness its collective intelligence.

Power is no longer a function of dominating the thinking and directing the work of others, it arises from being connected more than it does from being in charge. The four practices are small, intimate pieces of work and yet also an expression of the epic nature of the challenge.

The practice of valiance is an act of putting ourselves at risk and learning to see the risk as a personal and social act rather than a life-threatening one to which our old brains are still orientated. The practice of awareness encourages us to connect, moment-by-moment, to our unfolding experience as it is embodied; to lead organizational life as an ongoing series of tests, probes and experiments. The practice of gentleness supports us in being in conflict without exerting force and allows us to be careful with ourselves, as we experience the breaking apart of our organizations. Finally, the practice of persistence keeps us connected and open despite the repetitive nature of our defeats and difficulties.

So, dear reader, in parting: we need a new story for our times that is told well enough to compete with the growth-through-control stories of the previous Industrial Age. I am not suggesting this book is that complete story, I am suggesting there are many of us who are hungry for something new and who are creating separate chapters of the new story.

We need to have faith in the invisible companionship offered by these others, to search them out and hear about their experiences. My hope for you, as you complete this book, is that you have, at least, begun to capture your own story. This is a story in which you are fearless and unwavering as an expression of your power; aware and gentle as an expression of your love; the story in which we are all Flawed...but Willing.

# NOTES

1 Reproduced with permission from a range of poetry by Neil Usher on his Workessence blog (2014) http://workessence.com/barefoot-in-the-heart-part-1/

2 Matthew Tutty shared the anecdote on Mozart and his sister in response to reading the first draft of the book

3 Principles from the self-organizing and cross-sector movement Corporate Rebels United (2014). http://corporaterebelsunited.com/principles-2/

4 Gennep, A. (1960) *The Rites of Passage*. London: Routledge

5 King, M.L. (1967) *Where Do We Go From Here?* 11th Annual Southern Christian Leadership Conference Atlanta, GA

6 Reproduced with permission from a range of articles on the Freedom from Command and Control blog (2012) http://freedomfromcommandandcontrol.com/2012/09/15/public-sector-porkies-my-10-years-of-lying/

7 Chapman, S. (2014) *Can Scorpions Smoke - Creative Adventures In the Corporate World*. Self published.

8 Reproduced with permission from a range of articles on the Challenger Spirit blog (2012) http://challengerspirit.relume.co.uk/profiles/blogs/responsibly-breaking-the-rules